THE MONOGRAPH SERIES

KWAN & ASSOCIATES

Selected and Current Works

關永康建築師有限公司作品選

KWAN & ASSOCIATES

Selected and Current Works

關永康建築師有限公司作品選

First published in Australia in 1998 by
The Images Publishing Group Pty Ltd
ACN 059 734 431
6 Bastow Place, Mulgrave, Victoria, 3170
Telephone (61 3) 9561 5544 Facsimile (61 3) 9561 4860
E-mail: books@images.com.au

ISBN 1 875498 84 2.

Edited by Stephen Dobney
Designed by The Graphic Image Studio Pty Ltd,
Mulgrave, Australia
Film by Pageset Pty Ltd
Printed in Hong Kong

The directors of Kwan & Associates would like to
express their gratitude to freelance writer Jo Doyle for
writing both the introduction and the project text for
this book.

Thanks also Sonia Chan, Personal Assistant to Dominic
Kwan, for coordinating the production of this book and
to Kwan & Associates' Graphic Department for the
cover design and layout input.

Contents   目錄

Introduction

Kwan & Associates

Kwan & Associates is a firm which has eschewed the representative, preferring the freedom of the innovative response to the mandatory blueprint of signature architecture, and this is clearly demonstrated by the diversity of design on the following pages. In this introduction, founder Dominic Kwan and directors Vincent Ng and Grace Cheng speak about the firm and its vision.

Dominic Kwan's career in architecture spans a quarter of a century. Under his direction, Kwan & Associates, the firm he founded in 1991, has expanded steadily and now has a workforce 200-strong and an impressive track record. Kwan has decided to celebrate his success by buying office space in Island Place, a prestigious development in North Point, Hong Kong designed by his company.

Kwan & Associates originally evolved from KNW Architects & Engineers Limited (KNW) which was established in 1979, also by Dominic Kwan. KNW received widespread recognition for its architectural achievements. The Hong Kong Institute of Architects awarded the firm the Silver Medal for Excellence in Architecture in 1983, 1984 and 1989, and the Certificate of Merit in 1987.

After the dissolution of KNW, most of the staff stayed on board and worked to complete major assignments such as Tai Po Hospital and Pristine Villa at Tao Fung Shan.

As Mr Kwan remarks perceptively, his career could serve as a paradigm for the rise of the local architectural practice in Hong Kong. In the 1960s and 1970s, the architectural scene was dominated by a core group of European firms. Patronage came from government and non-Chinese developers, the mighty "hongs". A handful of first-generation "local" practices existed but they were awarded few prestigious projects.

By the mid-1970s, however, local players were beginning to carve an industry niche for themselves; firms established by local architects were on the rise and developers Li Ka Shing and Lee Shau Kee were laying the foundations of their now billion-dollar enterprises. Established at the end of that decade, KNW represented the second generation of local architects. This group may have had things slightly easier than its predecessors, but in the fiercely competitive climate, talent was not enough to succeed: skilful project management was vital. And this is still the case today.

This reflects the cut-throat nature of the building industry here. Both the developer and the architect are hampered by Hong Kong's physical and financial constraints. The dearth of space and a fast-growing population have resulted in a high-density built environment.

I asked Dominic Kwan why he feels that the industry here is so different from elsewhere.

"Limited land resources have created two major constraints on development: space and time. In such an environment, a developer must have entrepreneurial skills if he is to succeed. By this, I mean he must operate within a limited time-frame. Land costs are obviously high, as are lending rates, so a project

引言

關永康建築師有限公司

關永康建築師有限公司著重創新意念的建築設計，儘量避免被固定建築模式或風格所規限，這點可從該公司歷年所設計的各個項目中清楚顯示。在此簡介中，公司的創辦人關永康先生、兩位董事吳永順先生及鄭恩瑩小姐將談及該公司的發展方向及對建築設計的看法。

關永康先生從事建築設計工作已超過二十五年，並於一九九一年創立關永康建築師有限公司。在他的領導下，公司得以穩步發展並取得驕人的業績，該公司目前擁有二百名員工。近期，關先生更在北角港運城購置寫字樓，而這幢大廈亦是該公司的其中一項出色的設計。

關永康建築師有限公司的前身是「關吳黃建築師•工程師有限公司」，關吳黃是由關永康於一九七九年創立，經過多年努力及發展，該公司的傑出表現很快便受到各方面的認同，並分別在一九八三、一九八四及一九八九年獲得香港建築師學會所頒發的優秀建築設計銀獎，與及在一九八七年獲頒優異獎項。其後關吳黃改組，關永康建築師有限公司正式成立，而大部份員工均留下來，並為該公司完成多項大型的建築項目，如大埔醫院與及位於道風山的曉翠山莊等。

關先生認為他的事業發展正好體現了香港建築師行業的變化。六、七十年代，外國公司在本地的建築師行業佔盡優勢，而政府及那些財雄勢大的外地發展商為最大的投資者。其中雖有小部份屬於第一代的本地建築師，但鮮能投得大型的發展項目。到了七十年代中，本地建築商相繼在香港建業市場冒起，而本地的建築師亦開始發展他們的事業，一些著名地產發展商如李嘉誠及李兆基等也就在此時建立現今龐大的基業。

關吳黃亦在這時期末創立，是本地的第二代建築師。此時期比以前發展較易，但仍要面對激烈的競爭環境，單憑個人的才能並不足夠，必須同時具備出色的工程管理技巧，而這點亦是現今在建築工程上備受重視的一環。

在香港從事建築工作存在一定困難，發展商和建築師皆受到地型及經濟發展所限制，而土地不足加上急速人口增長更造成高密度的建築環境。

我詢問關永康先生為何認為這裡的建築業跟其他地方有所不同？

「有限的土地資源對建築業發展造成了兩項嚴重的局限：空間及時間，要在這種環境下生存，發展商須擁有企業性策略，即在有限的時間及高土地成本的環境下，儘快完成工程。再者，高密度及高速樓宇發展使大部份的建築物皆有著相同的建築模式，而直立式設計更是無可避免的，雖然這並不一定會帶來負面的影響。」

must be completed as quickly as possible. In addition, high-density and high-speed developments have resulted in a built environment composed of repetitive building forms; vertical development is unavoidable, although this is not necessarily a negative phenomenon."

Fellow director Vincent Ng agrees. For him, the challenge is to develop interest within these narrow parameters: "The environment we operate in calls for large-scale developments to be designed and built in a very short time. A good architect needs to work quickly yet meticulously. Such restrictions encourage innovation."

Grace Cheng, for her part, feels that the opportunities for architects here are phenomenal: "Millions of square feet go up each year, so the architect has plenty of opportunity to hone his or her craft. In other major cities, the built environment has evolved slowly over time and there is little opportunity to design a landmark building or to significantly alter the fabric of the city."

When asked what changes they would like to see in the future, all three agree that improvements in the construction industry are much needed.

"Regrettably," says Dominic Kwan, "construction practices here are very low-tech. There are a few prime development exceptions, but on the whole, high-volume, fast-paced construction has left little time for the development of cutting-edge technology. Recently, the Port and Airport Development Strategy programme necessitated the importation, and indeed the development, of innovative civil engineering techniques; we should like to see such innovation across all types of construction."

Kwan believes that government must accept much of the blame for this situation since, through the quasi-government Housing Authority, it puts up more than 50 per cent of the residences in Hong Kong yet has so far been reluctant to exert any pressure on the industry. He feels that this is because, in the past, quantity has been prioritised over quality. This has resulted in both inferior construction and a lack of interest in research and development.

"In Japan, architects work with manufacturers to produce the latest in cladding or energy-efficient glass. Here, we rely on importing second-hand technology. I am confident, however, that China will one day make provision for our research and development needs," he continues.

Is this interest in technological advancement articulated in the designs of Kwan & Associates?

"Whereas we are keen to use the latest design techniques," answers Grace Cheng, "the firm has avoided the adoption of a distinctive house style. We feel that each project should be treated innovatively, and that creativity should draw on the team's diverse experiences and insights."

However, at the core of any design response, she stresses, is the exploration of strategic options, the exploitation of site schemes, and consultation with field professionals.

Why the emphasis on experiential insight?

"It allows us," explains Ng, "to use our individual sensitivities to respond to the different environments in each case.

董事吳永順先生亦贊同這觀點，吳先生認為在這種備受限制的環境下發展業務是一項極大的挑戰：

「這裡的環境促使我們進行多項大型的發展計劃，並且能在極短時間內完成。一個優秀的建築師必須要有高的工作效率和嚴謹的態度，至於那種種限制反而會引發創新的設計意念。」

董事鄭恩瑩小姐則覺得建築師在世界各地均能找到發展機會：「每年有數以百萬呎計算的樓宇落成，為建築師提供了很多一展所長的機會。但在其他主要城市，建築環境往往要隨著時間慢慢發展，故此，較少機會可以設計一座具有特色的建築物或將整個城市建築風格改變。」

當問及他們希望將來建築業有何發展時，三位不約而同地認為建築技術必須作出一定的改進。

關先生表示：「我覺得很遺憾，現時香港的建築技術明顯較為落後，只有幾項重要的大型發展工程能達到一定的水平，相信這是由於整個建築業的高產量及快速生產步伐，造成根本沒有時間發展及改良建築技術。最近，港口及機場發展計劃引進了不少嶄新的土木工程技術，而我們期望這些新穎的技術可以逐步應用於其他的各項建築工程上。

在日本，建築師可以與製造商攜手製造最新穎的覆面建材或有節能作用的玻璃，但本地的建築師卻只能採用外來的科技。不過，我相信未來國內將能為我們提供這方面的研究和發展資源。」

你們公司的設計是否均考慮與先進技術互相配合，以達到最佳的效果？

鄭恩瑩小姐回應：「我們熱衷採用最新的科技設計，而公司亦盡量避免定下某種固定的建築模式，因為每項工程應盡量注入新鮮的創作意念，並需源於每位設計者的不同經驗及獨到的眼光。」

不過她強調任何設計均要利用選擇性的策略加上完善的工程計劃，更要諮詢業內專業人士的意見。

為甚麼特別強調從經驗得來的獨到眼光？

吳永順先生解釋：「憑著過往經驗使我們能對不同的情況作出靈活的處理方法，其中要考慮的因素包括客戶、城市規劃以及用家各方面。我們對某些情況所作出的即時回應可作為參考，以便最後能定出更佳的方案。」

故此建築師必須就各種情況作出不同的處理方法，而不能只沿用著同一種模式。關先生認為可幸的是公司並沒有墨守成規，一成不變的建築師。

By environment I mean the client, the urban setting and the end user. Our reaction to these various contexts is initially tentative, but enables us to formulate a response which embraces many factors."

By its very nature, this code prohibits a premeditated response to a brief. Kwan remarks that he is proud that the firm doesn't have a ubiquitous "signature" architect.

"The company thinks in bigger terms than just one person. There is an emphasis on teamwork and shared experience. A signature architect is less sustainable than a team with collective goals. And, importantly, regeneration is always possible with a team."

Adds Ng: "There is room for the expression of personality in our work but the designer will never overwhelm the design. In addition, our portfolio is very diverse. A firm can't have a single statement articulated across residential, cultural, commercial, medical and religious buildings—each category has its own requirements. Imposition can be very negative; our watchwords are "listen" and "react", thereby generating a design which is absolutely sensitive."

Exhaustive post-mortems after a project is completed, and at various intervals thereafter, create feedback which, in turn, promotes a culture of sharing within the firm. "We have 200 people here; one person can't do everything," Cheng points out.

The firm's designs are particularly conscious of the needs of the end user. There is a clear refusal to position technology or professional training above human needs. This is evidenced by designs such as the Ko Shan Theatre or the Hung Shui Kui residential development, which allow open dialogue between landscape and interior. Ng explains that when they are devising a scheme, they will visit a site simply to "experience" the place: "The designers are encouraged to react emotively. If impressed by the surrounding greenery, they should bring it into the design. This may not be the strictly logical response, but it is a human response and so acknowledges the end user."

Although the firm keeps abreast of current trends in the global architectural scene, it refuses to follow slavishly a particular school of thought, preferring instead to react to different elements from assorted theories. "For our architects," concludes Ng, "innovation is everywhere. Everyday images or objects will be as readily incorporated into a scheme as a philosophy or movement. The Maybank project in Singapore, for instance, recalls a mobile phone—an appropriate reference for Hong Kong architects."

In the final analysis, however, the firm's insistence on meeting budgets, completing designs on time and ensuring that construction is equally timely have been as crucial to its success as its design skills. In Hong Kong, perhaps more so than anywhere else, time is money, as any successful practice knows.

Jo Doyle is managing editor of the Hong Kong magazine *Building Journal* and a freelance writer.

「建築設計工作著重團隊精神，強調集體創作及彼此分享經驗。單獨一個建築師獨力去處理各項工作自然不及群體的力量。」

吳永順先生補充：「集體工作的環境既可讓設計師發揮所長，同時亦可避免局限了設計的意念。再者，公司所擁有的多元化工程項目，均有著個別不同的要求，例如：住宅、藝術、商業、醫療或宗教等，故建築師不能一成不變地用同一設計模式或去處理所有的建築項目。因此，我們必須細心考慮不同項目的性質及要求，務求令設計作品能真正切合實際用途。」

當每項工程完成後，均會作出檢討，而負責該工程的建築師亦會就有關的細節及過程互相交流經驗，使其他人均能從中得益，並作為以後處理同類工程的參考，而這種經驗交流在建築設計上是非常有用的。

該公司的設計尤其著重用戶的需要，強調客人的需要應是首要的考慮因素，甚至在科技或專業訓練之上。關於這點，在高山劇場或洪水橋住宅發展設計中可以表現出來，我們可以看到室外環境與室內佈置如何透過巧妙的設計而達至高度的協調。吳永順先生解釋，當他們策劃一個工程時，會先到地盤巡察，以便作實地瞭解。「設計師必須要有敏銳的觸覺，細心觀察周圍的事物及環境，並把它融合於設計中。這種對四周環境的直接感覺，是人類與生俱來的自然反應，將有助設計者了解用戶的相同感受及需要。」

雖然公司一向密切注意全球最新建築面貌及趨勢，但卻不會盲目仿效，反而會綜合各種理論的元素而作出不同回應。吳永順總結道：「對於建築師而言，創作靈感俯拾皆是。每日見到的影像或事物都可演化成理論或元素，並成為建築師其中一項參考資料，應用於各項發展計劃之中。如新加坡的馬來西亞銀行工程就令人聯想到流動無線電話的外型。」

最後，總結公司成功要素，除了出色的設計技巧外，妥善的時間分配，按步就班地處理各項工序，並能準時完成有關工程，以達致最佳成本效益，是公司一貫做事的方式，而相比其他地方，香港的建築業者更明白時間就是金錢的道理。

Jo Doyle 是香港建築雜誌 Building Journal 的執行編輯及業餘作家

Selected and Current Works

作　品　選

Ko Shan Theatre

Design/Completion 1993/1996
Ko Shan Park, Hung Hom, Kowloon, Hong Kong
Urban Council
2,200 square metres (existing);
2,240 square metres (new)
Reinforced concrete
Metal panels, aluminium curtain wall,
glass, granite

高山劇場擴建工程

設計年份/完成年份：1993年/1996年
區域市政局
紅磡高山道公園
建築面積：2,200平方米(原有)，
2,240平方米(新建)
建築材料：鋼筋混凝土、金屬板、鋁幕牆、
玻璃、花崗岩石

1

This project involved a renovation and rebuild
to replace an open-air auditorium which was
unsuited to the climate. The new wing, which is
married to the existing theatre and site context,
provides an entrance lobby, a ticketing office,
exhibition space, a cafeteria with roof garden,
office space and rehearsal suites.

Functions within the wing are organised around
a free-flowing promenade with an oval foyer and
staircase at its centre which act as exhibition
hall and spatial connection with the first floor
lobby. This space is topped by a convex oval
skylight.

The concept of "theatre in the park" is expressed
through the use of reflective glass and
aluminium panels to both mirror the park in the
facade and create a continuum with the interior
where these materials continue to formulate a
sequence of dynamic spaces.

The elevation is dressed in a lightweight metal
frame which declares its kinship with the
concrete curvilinear form and capped roof
of the existing theatre. At specific junctures,
such as the entrance, the frame is modulated
for emphasis.

這是一項修葺及重建工程，以取代一個不適宜香港氣候
的露天表演場地。新翼與現有劇場及觀眾席渾然一體，
設有劇場入口大堂、售票處、展覽場地、自助餐廳、
辦公室及彩排間。

新翼內部的各種設施，沿寬闊的走興建廊佈置，中央為
一個橢圓形的大堂及樓梯間，用作展覽廳及連接二樓
大堂的空間。中央大堂頂，採用橢圓形凸面設計，增加
採光效果，配以天藍色燈光。

"園中劇場"這個構思，則透過反光玻璃和鋁板達成。
反光玻璃和鋁板把公園景色映射到劇場的正面，與劇場
的室內景緻連貫在一起，相映成趣，形成一系列動感
空間景象。同時室內空間更技巧地與外圍境緊密連在
一起。

劇場新翼的立面，採用輕質金屬框裝飾，使新翼的
氣派，與現有劇場的混凝土曲線形狀及帽式屋頂迴異。
為了使效果更加鮮明，這種輕質金屬框的轉變位置，
設在特定的接合部位如入口處。

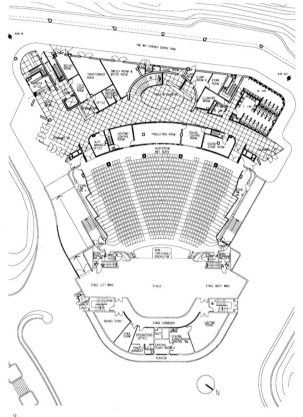

NEW WING
(ADDITION)
新翼

OLD WING
(ALTERATION)
舊翼

2

1   Theatre in the park
2   Ground floor plan
3   Modulated frame of main entrance
4   Convex oval skylight

1   園中劇場
2   地面平面圖
3   正人口拱門
4   橢圓形凸面天窗

3

4

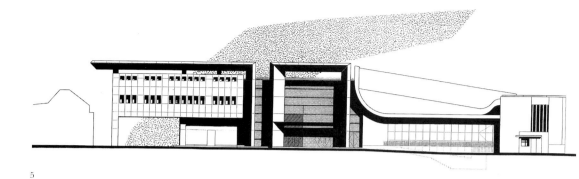

5

6

7

8

11

9

10

12

13

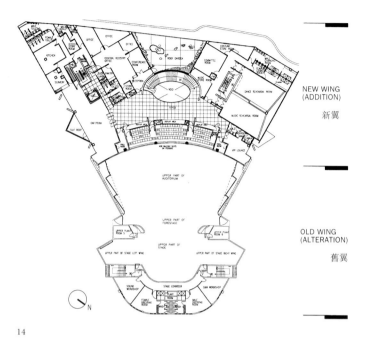

NEW WING
(ADDITION)

新翼

OLD WING
(ALTERATION)

舊翼

14

16

17

15

18

19

20

21

22

23

24

Maybank Chambers

Design 1997
2 Battery Road, Singapore
Maybank
13,930 square metres
Reinforced concrete
Curtain wall, aluminium panels

馬來西亞銀行新加坡總部大廈

設計年份：1997 年
2 Battery Road, Singapore
馬來西亞銀行
建築面積：15,690 平方米
建築材料：幕牆、鋁板材

When viewed from the sea, Singapore's cityscape is dominated by tall buildings of eclectic disposition. This 34-storey tower unites both office and banking space in a dynamic geometric form in the urban waterfront context—a context which it respects while distinguishing itself as a progressive financial institution.

The street scale in Fullerton Square is maintained by the height of the podium, which corresponds to the roof level of the adjacent historic Fullerton House. The proportions of the colonnade outside the banking hall also paraphrase the older structure. The use of contemporary materials such as cladding and glazing, however, reflects the spirit of the age. Likewise, the uniquely curved body of the tower is set back to maintain the urban scale while revitalising the square.

An open corner facing Cavenagh Bridge addresses the Singapore River and receives the pedestrian flow. As both office entrance and bank hall demand street access, and to maximise useable area and individual entrance space, vertical segregation of use is introduced to the podium. The banking hall's three-storey entrance atrium connects it to the outdoor space and scale; it is fully glazed to allow maximum transparency. The office lobby also fronts Fullerton Square. Above, the office core is planned along Flint Street, generating a panoramic sea view for users.

This project was designed in association with Singapore's SYL Architects.

從海上遠眺新加坡的城市輪廓，主要由形態不一的高樓大廈構成。這座34層高的辦公室及銀行業務兩用途大廈，以動感的幾何形狀矗立在市區的岸邊－既與其莊重的城市輪廓融為一體，又保持其作為一家先進的金融機構應備的特徵。

大廈位於Fullerton Square，其平台高度與毗鄰的歷史名廈Fullerton House的屋頂看齊，而銀行大堂外的柱廊比例，亦與毗鄰舊廈相稱，使大廈與該區的城市輪廓相配合。但是，大廈採用的各種現代建築材料，例如嵌板材料及玻璃，與及大廈獨特的曲線形主體，卻反映出時代的氣息，更賦予廣場新的活力。

大廈面向Cavenagh Bridge的一面設有一片開放式空間，與新加坡河呼應，並可容納往來的人流。而低座平台採用垂直分隔方式設計，除了為辦公大樓及銀行業務大廳提供主要入口通道外，亦同時得到最大的可用面積和獨立的入口空間。銀行業務大廳及入口大堂的三層高中庭，採用玻璃幕牆，讓大廳與室外空間連接，並得到最佳的景觀。而大廈背靠Flint Street排列，使用戶可以飽覽美麗海景。

這項作品，由關永康建築師有限公司與新加坡司徒宇亮建築繪測師合作，並在公開設計比賽中榮獲冠軍。

1

4

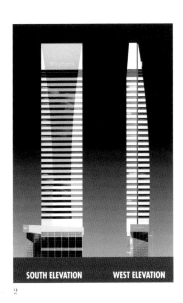

SOUTH ELEVATION   WEST ELEVATION

2

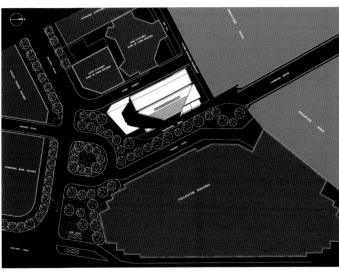

5

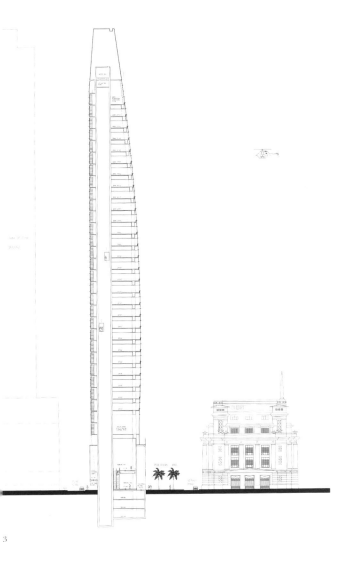

3

6

Methodist Church

Design/Completion 1993/1997
Wanchai, Hong Kong
New World Development/The Methodist Church
7,920 square metres
Reinforced concrete
Granite, ceramic tiles, aluminium windows

循道衛理聯合教會香港堂

設計年份 / 完成年份：1993 年 /1997 年
香港灣仔
新世界發展 / 循道衛理聯合教會
建築面積：7,287 平方米
建築材料：鋼筋混凝土、花崗岩石、
瓷磚 、鋁窗

1

This project, a redevelopment of a 1930s Methodist church, combines ecclesiastical functions with a 24-storey office tower on a small, triangular island site. The church is positioned at the site apex, parallel to the busy Hennessy Road, and is the focal point of the development. Inside, the alignment of the sanctuary altar along the same axis reinforces this focus.

Red granite cladding recalls the brickwork of the original church, as does the enscripted glass fenestration and new spire. The bell tower is also reintroduced, but now a beacon lures the faithful.

The sanctuary is accessed via a staircase which ascends a double-height circular entrance lobby with mezzanine gallery. The client wished to modernise church practices to take account of social and technological change. Consequently, although the 11-metre-high sanctuary accommodates only 500 worshippers, a video wall broadcasts the service in a chapel above, effectively doubling the church's capacity. A video suite is included to allow services to be recorded.

An efficient marriage between the scheme's two seemingly contradictory components was vital. The exterior treatment of the office tower is based on graduated vertical forms in varying colours which complement the church facade. However, a curved window wall dominates the central axis, creating its own identity. In response to different user schedules, the lobby and lift core are shared but the church and office space have individual entrances.

2

該工程項目是將一所三十年代的循道衛理教會教堂，重建成一幢能保持原有教堂功能的24層高辦公室大樓。建築物位於軒尼詩道與莊士敦道交界處的三角形土地上，外型別樹一格的教堂建於低層部份，亦是整項建築的焦點，而教堂內殿設計則按照該建築物相同軸線處理，以突出其重心所在。

教堂以紅色花崗岩覆面，令人聯想到原教堂的磚牆色調，再襯以手繪裝飾玻璃門窗及重新配置的尖頂鐘樓，為建築物營造出一種莊嚴敬虔的形象。

由教堂正門的圓形入口大堂及長廊可直達主堂的聖殿。同時，為了配合未來的科技發展及客戶的要求，教堂內更設有錄影室設備，以便將崇拜活動過程錄影下來，再投映在聖堂上的一幅視像幕牆上，令原只可容納500名信徒的聖堂，其參與人數得以倍增。

這項重建計劃的關鍵之處，是要把兩種功能各異的元素放置在一起，為達致兩方面的和諧，辦公室大樓的外牆部份乃採用與教堂相襯的顏色，並綴以相稱的垂直圖案，而大樓中央的一組弧形窗壁，更是別具風格。此外，為配合不同的需要，除大堂及電梯是共同使用，教堂部份和辦公室大樓均各自設有獨立的入口。

3

4

5

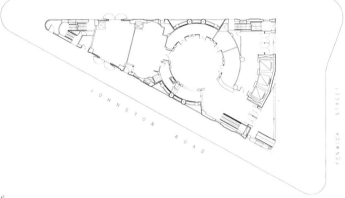

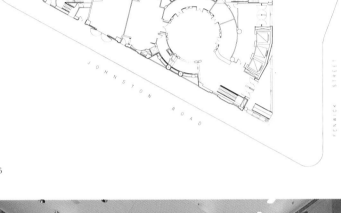

6

7

8

9

10

St Francis Church

Design/Completion 1992/1996
Ma On Shan, New Territories, Hong Kong
The Bishop of the Roman Catholic Church
in Hong Kong
2,450 square metres
Reinforced concrete post and beam structure
Black anodised aluminium window wall,
ceramic mosaic tiles, reinforced concrete,
stained glass, marble, stone, timber

馬鞍山天主教聖方濟堂

設計年份 / 完成年份：1992 年 /1996 年
香港新界馬鞍山
天主教香港教區
建築面積：2,450 平方米
建築結構：鋼筋混凝土柱樑結構
建築材料：黑色鋁窗、彩色瓷磚、鋼筋水泥、
彩色玻璃、雲石、石料、木料

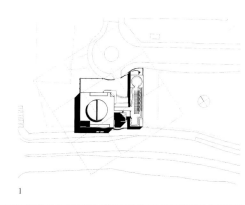

1

The church, located in a residential district, is built to reflect the neighbourhood scale. The project accommodates a chapel, a multipurpose hall, an office, function rooms and priest's quarters.

The two main spaces are housed in a square block, with the remaining spaces in a long, rectangular block. The two blocks lie perpendicular to each other, connected by a tall, rectangular volume which serves as a spire. A clear glass curtain wall facade communicates the circulatory system within.

Hard geometric forms have been softened by the inclusion of curves and colour, such as the red curvilinear wall on the corner of the function block. A circular opening in the canopy above the main entrance creates a "crown of sky" through which visitors pass in a metaphorical baptism of light.

The interior of the chapel is laid out along a diagonal axis so that the pews radiate out from the altar and the congregation is not segregated from the priest.

該項工程包括興建一座聖堂、一個多用途禮堂、一個辦事處、多間活動室及神父起居室。由於該教堂座落於一個住宅區內，建築師於是運用巧妙的技巧，使建築物能夠反映出鄰里比例。

聖堂和多用途禮堂這兩項主要設施置於一座正方形大樓內，其餘設施設在一座長方形樓宇內。兩座建築物直角相交，並由一座長方形高塔連接。而主樓梯外則採用透明玻璃幕牆，使樓宇內的人流系統互相配合。

建築物硬朗的幾何建築設計，被各種曲線和顏色(例如長方形樓宇轉角處的紅色弧面牆)加以柔化。教堂主入口上蓋的圓洞，隱喻訪客行經這裏時，接受天父之光的沐浴。

聖堂內的各項設施，沿一條對角軸線佈置，長凳以祭台為中心向外伸展排列，讓教友圍著神父而坐，加強內聚感。

2

3

4

5

6

7

8

9

10

Hing Wai Building

Design/Completion 1994/1997
Queen's Road, Central, Hong Kong
Hing Wai Investment Company
6,846 square metres
Reinforced concrete
Laminated glass, granite, aluminium windows

興瑋大廈

設計年份 / 完成年份：1994 年 /1997 年
香港皇后大道中
興瑋投資公司
建築面積：6,840 平方米
建築材料：鋼筋混凝土、疊層玻璃、
花崗岩石、鋁窗

This commercial tower occupies a prominent yet restrictive corner site and comprises a four-storey retail component with 20 office floors above. To distinguish itself from its more monolithic neighbours, the tower is built to its site limits; the elevation rises from street level and addresses the intersection of Queen's Road and D'Aguilar Street, emphasising its verticality. Use has also been made of the open space fronting the neighbouring Entertainment Building to improve sight lines to the building.

The tower further accents this corner location, with a spine of curved glazing above the monumental entrance. This spine, with its multi-shaded, laminated fenestration, articulates the stonework of the elevation.

Office space is arranged around a central atrium which rises to the twentieth floor; an L-shaped plan is then adopted to taper the mass of the building. The atrium filters diffused sunlight into the office units and provides another visual experience for office users, who benefit from this ancillary interior elevation.

這幢商業大廈位處一個備受局限的角落位置，由四層的購物商場及十九層的辦公室大樓所組成。該大廈用盡了地盤的全部地面，其立面由街面升起，屹立於皇后大道與德己笠街交界處，令其筆直宏偉的外型比鄰近的樓宇更為突出。而設計上亦利用了面對毗鄰娛樂行騰出的地面空間，以改善該大廈的視覺形像。

為了進一步突出其所在的角落位置，正門入口上方特別設計了一根弧形玻璃柱體，並由多層陰影色調及層疊式門窗佈局，更加突顯建築物立面的石體結構。

大廈內的寫字樓單位，圍繞著一個延伸至二十樓的中央光井部份，加上L形的平面佈局，能大大舒緩了大廈的壓迫感。柔和的陽光更可經中央光井部份散射進室內，令用戶可感受到這種由室內輔助立面處理所帶來的視覺體驗。

1

2

3

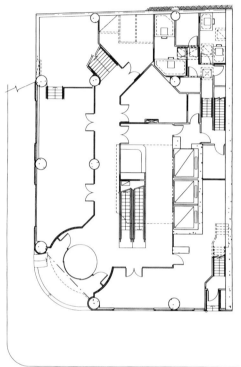

4

5

6

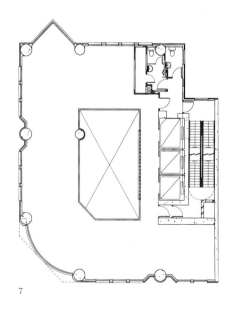

7

Star of the Sea Church

Design/Completion 1994/1995
Chai Wan, Hong Kong
The Bishop of the Roman Catholic Church in
Hong Kong
814 square metres
Reinforced concrete
Natural stone and timber (interior)

海星堂室內設計

設計年份 / 完成年份：1994 年 /1995 年
香港柴灣
天主教香港教區
建築面積：814 平方米
建築材料：鋼筋混凝土、天然石塊及木料(室內)

This project involved the interior fitting out of
a church complex.

A semi-open courtyard fronting the chapel serves
as a transition space where worshippers can
either contemplate spiritual matters before
entering or congregate after Mass. A central
font symbolises baptism into the Church.
The adjacent prayer room houses a tabernacle
in a space dedicated to prayer and meditation.
Two confessionals are also located here.

A recurring cruciform Chinese motif generates
visual cohesion between the courtyard, prayer
room and chapel. Inside the chapel, the pews
fan out from the altar, reducing the distance
between congregation and priest. The original
altar stone, saved from the demolished church
which occupied the same site, forms the
foundation for the new altar. Symbolism
abounds: steps in front of the ambo signify the
elevation of the liturgy; a skylight over the
sanctuary infuses the space with natural light,
suggesting God's presence; the rear wall is a
memorial for the departed; and the side walls
are punctuated with 14 clerestory windows
depicting the Stations of the Cross.

Natural materials and warm tones further
enhance the spiritual ambience.

本項工程為一座教堂的室內設計。

一個面對教堂的半露天前庭，用作過渡空間，可讓信眾
在進入教堂前，在這裡靜思祈禱，亦可讓他們在完成
彌撒後，於這裡聚集。前庭中央的洗禮池，象徵及提醒
信眾是經過洗禮而進入教會的。毗鄰的祈禱室內，
提供了為祈禱及默想專用的地方，內設有一座神龕及
兩間修和室。

一個十字形的中式漏窗圖型，在前庭、祈禱室和教室內
重覆地使用，把這三個地方的設計貫連起來。教堂內，
教堂長凳從祭壇向外以扇形排列，使信眾與神父之間的
距離拉近，亦產生一種內聚感。原來位於該地點，
被拆除的教堂原有的祭台，現用作新祭台的台面石，
使海星堂的歷史延續下去。

室內的設計手法亦包含了各種象徵意義：如讀經台前
的步階，可增加禮儀感的同時亦表達聖言的重要性，
教堂內一個方形的天窗，能把自然光引入室內，象徵天
主的存在；後牆是亡者紀念碑，讓信友為故人祈禱；
而側牆上開有十四個高窗，象徵主耶穌被釘十字架前
所經歷的十四處路。各種天然材料的和暖色調，進一步
加強教堂的和諧而 神聖氣氛。

1   Floor plan
2   The chapel with pews encircling the altar
3   Elevation
4   Baptismal font
5   Stained glass window inside prayer room
6   Chinese motif in grotto
7   Sanctuary

1   平面圖
2   環繞祭台排列的信眾座位
3   立面圖
4   聖洗池
5   祈禱室內的彩色玻璃窗
6   聖母岩的梅花圖型
7   聖所

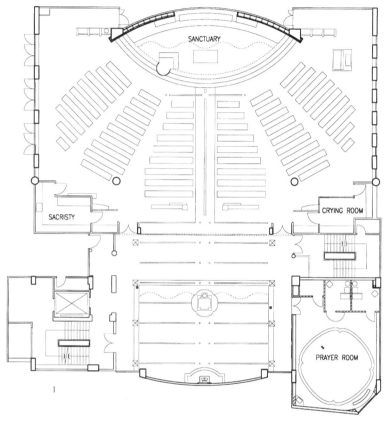

1

2

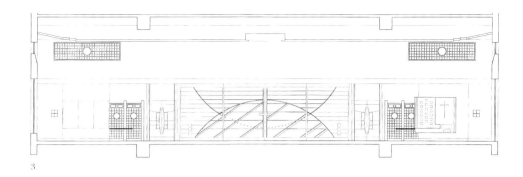

3

4

5

6

7

Kowloon Station Development

Design/Completion 1996/2005
West Kowloon, Hong Kong
Mass Transit Railway Corporation (MTRC)
Consultants: Terry Farrell & Partners,
Ove Arup & Partners, Chapman Taylor Partners
1,090,026 square metres
Reinforced concrete
Granite cladding, aluminium cladding, ceramic
tiles, glass curtain wall

機場九龍車站發展計劃

設計年份 / 完成年份：1996 年 /2005 年
香港西九龍
香港地下鐵路公司
顧問：Terry Farrell & Partners, 奧雅納工程顧問,
Chapman Taylor
建築面積：1,090,026 平方米
建築材料：鋼筋混凝土、花崗岩覆面板、鋁覆面、
瓷磚、幕牆

Occupying a gigantic 135,517-square-metre
footprint, the Kowloon Station development
is a mixed-use project comprising 23 podium-
mounted towers connected at basement level to
the new MTRC Lantau Railway Kowloon Station.

The mammoth development will accommodate
office towers, hotels, residential towers, a
shopping mall and a transport interchange.
A total of 5,050 residential units have been
planned. The 87-storey landmark office/hotel
building will be the joint tallest building in the
SAR (Special Administrative Region).

The architects have been nominated as
Authorised Person and have responsibility for
the residential component of the project.

這項龐大的綜合發展項目佔地135,517平方米，包括建於
基座平台上的23幢建築物，其底層部份將與地下鐵路
九龍車站相連。

該大型的結構工程設有辦公室大樓、酒店、住宅物業、
大型購物中心及交通中轉站，計劃中住宅項目將提供
5,050個住宅單位，另外一幢約87層高的辦公/酒店大樓
建成後，將成為全港最高的建築物之一。

整個住宅項目的建築設計部份及認可人仕職責均由
建築師負責。

1

1   Site plan
2   The first stage of the development consists of six
    residential towers and a podium-level residents'
    club at the heart of the site

1   位置圖
2   位處於中心地帶的第一期住宅發展包括6幢住宅及住客會所

2

Kowloon Station Development, First Development Package

Design/Completion 1996/1999
West Kowloon, Hong Kong
Mass Transit Railway Corportation (MTRC)/
Union Charm Development Ltd
147,562 square metres
Reinforced concrete
Granite cladding, aluminium cladding,
ceramic tiles, curtain wall

This development consists of six residential towers which house a total of 1,300 units. The top quality apartments range in size from 70 to 232 square metres.

The towers, which adopt a modified cruciform plan, ascend from a podium which has basement car parking space, a public transport terminus at ground floor level, and government and social facilities at the first floor. The podium deck is attractively landscaped and is overlooked by a residents' clubhouse located on the first floor of the tower. This club, with an articulated, curved landscaped roof, acts as a buffer zone between the residential towers and the car parking facilities.

The development is an updated application of the long-established and necessary Hong Kong practice of efficient usage of transport and service infrastructure.

機場九龍車站發展計劃：
第一期發展項目

設計年份/完成年份：1996年/1999年
香港西九龍
香港地下鐵路公司/永泰亞洲集團
建築面積：147,562平方米
建築材料：花崗岩覆面板、鋁覆面、瓷磚、幕牆

機鐵九龍車站第一期發展項目包括6幢住宅樓宇，提供1,300個面積由70至232平方米的高級住宅單位。

各住宅大樓用經過改良的十字形設計，其基座是一個平台花園，平台內設有地庫及停車場，地面一層為公共交通工具總站，二樓則用作社會服務設施。住宅大廈二樓的住客會所以弧形的頂部及園藝裝飾，藉以分隔住宅大廈與停車場部份，並作為一個緩衝地帶，與平台花園同樣產生美化環境的作用。

這項發展項目正好體現了香港長久以來善用交通及服務設施的結構，成為最具效益的物業發展計劃。

1   Perspective

1   透視圖

1

The University of Hong Kong Phase 5 Redevelopment

Design/Completion 1991/1995
University of Hong Kong, Pokfulam, Hong Kong
University of Hong Kong
13,632 square metres
Reinforced concrete post and beam structure
Black anodised aluminium window wall, tinted glazing, drywall partitions, ironspot clay external wall tiles

香港大學重建第五期教學大樓

設計年份／完成年份：1991 年／1995 年
香港薄扶林香港大學
香港大學
建築面積：13,632 平方米
建築結構：鋼筋混凝土柱樑結構
建築材料：黑色陽極化鋁質窗牆、顏色玻璃、鐵斑粘土外牆瓷磚、大樓隔板

1

This development accommodates the university's Engineering Department. Sited on a slope bounded by greenery and fronting onto Victoria Harbour, the building is planned to exploit its situation. Circulation mechanisms, service space, lecture rooms and laboratories are organised around the central axis, and administration and tuition space flanks the north and south edges of the rectangular volume. Drywall partitions enable spatial flexibility.

The main campus of the University manifests three main building types from across the twentieth century. This diversity of vocabulary and period is articulated in the design of the Chow Yei Ching Building through elements such as projecting columns, horizontal ribbon windows, external frames, brises soleil and bay windows. Shades of brown were chosen for the elevation to harmonise with the campus profile, while overlaid bands of silver denote ascent and modernity.

Due to a lack of access at street level, the entrance, a two-storey lobby with glass window wall, is reached via adjacent facilities.

這座為香港大學工程系教學大樓座落在綠化帶山坡上，正面俯覽維多利亞海港，環境優美。人流系統、活動空間、演講室及實驗室，圍繞大樓中軸排列；行政及教授之辦公室則位於矩形樓的南北兩端。大樓內採用隔板分隔，使空間可以靈活更改。

香港大學的主校園，由跨越二十世紀的三種主要類型的樓宇組成。設計周亦卿樓(Chow Yei Ching Building)時，利用各種構件，例如突柱、水平拉窗、外靈框架、百葉窗及凸窗，把不同時期及多種類型的建築特色銜接起來。大樓選用褐色為主色，與校園的色調和諧配合，而外牆的銀色飾帶，則令大樓顯現高雅及現代的氣息。

大樓的入口大堂樓高兩層，裝設透明玻璃幕牆，由於地形關係，無法在地面興建入口，因此，須由相鄰的樓宇進入這座大堂。

2

Key
1   Sitting Area
2   Lift Lobby
3   Undergraduate Lab. 1
4   Undergraduate Lab. 2
5   AHU Room
6   Cleaner Store
7   Instruction Lab.
8   Lecture Theatre B
9   Lecture Theatre C
10 Lobby
11 Toilet

3

7

4

8

9

5

6

10

Tai Yu Square

Design/Completion 1994/1998
Beijing, China
Tai Yu International Investment Group Ltd
316,200 square metres
Reinforced concrete
Granite, curtain wall

北京台友廣場

設計年份/完成年份：1994年/1998年
中國北京
台友國際投資集團有限公司
建築面積：302,220平方米(94.8.15版)
建築材料：花崗岩石、幕牆

1

The project is a multi-use development incorporating residential and commercial elements, including a hotel, bank tower, office tower, shopping arcade and private club. These distinct components are separated by a road network: the commercial blocks stand adjacent to the main street, while the four residential towers are located in a green setting at the quieter northern end of the site, linked to the shopping arcade by a footbridge.

The commercial towers vary markedly in height and massing to reflect their functional differences and to generate visual interest. The surface treatment of the towers concentrates on the use of various types of glass and granite at different levels to enrich the facades' fabric and texture. A series of horizontal elements articulates the corners.

Natural lighting is central to the design of the shopping arcade, effecting a continuum with the outside while also emphasising shelter; this space becomes the *genus loci* of the retail podium. A glazed skylit arcade links the central atrium to the other commercial activities, reiterating the outdoor connection.

這是一個商住兩用的綜合發展項目，包括一座酒店、銀行中心、辦公大樓、購物商場、私人會所以及四座住宅塔樓。這些各具特色的建築物，由道路網清楚劃分。各幢商業大樓及酒店靠近大街位置，而四座住宅則座落於其北 端的一片綠化區內，並有行人天橋連接相鄰的購物商場。

各幢商業大樓的高度不一、大小有別，不但反映其不同之功能，亦能產生視覺美感。建築物的表面處理是在不同層次，採用各種玻璃和花崗岩飾面石板，使樓宇外表紋理更見豐富。

在購物商場的設計上，中庭部分採用自然採光，使商場作為室內購物場所之餘，也能與室外景觀互相銜接。一道裝有玻璃天窗上蓋的連拱廊，把中庭與其它商業部分連接起來，使中庭成為裙樓商場的交通樞紐及中心。

2

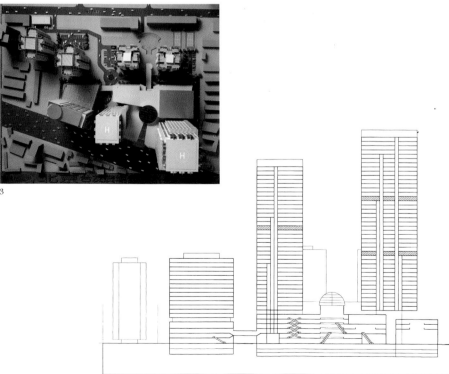

3

1 Typical floor plan
2 Perspective
3 Bird's-eye view
4 Schematic section

1 標準層平面圖
2 透視圖
3 模型鳥瞰
4 示意剖面圖

4

Shanghai Ding Feng Plaza

Design/Completion 1995/1998
Jiading, Shanghai, China
JG Summit Holdings Inc.
60,000 square metres
Reinforced concrete
Ceramic tiles, spray paint

上海頂峰廣場

設計年份 / 完成年份：1995 年 /1998 年
中國上海嘉定
建築面積：60,000 平方米
建築材料：鋼筋混凝土、瓷磚、噴漆

1

As the first phase of a comprehensive multi-use project, this six-storey commercial development comprises a shopping arcade, a six-screen cinema complex, a food court, restaurants, karaoke venues, a department store and a bowling alley.

Built to a rectilinear plan, the retail arcade is located at the front part of the building and is organised around three distinctive skylit voids which flood the space with natural light. The remaining commercial and entertainment activities are located at the south-western side of the complex.

The focus of the facade is the main entrance, which is clearly marked with a large, energetic advertising board. The elevation is further ornamented with horizontal and vertical elements which introduce a more human scale to this massive retail volume.

頂峰廣場是一項綜合性物業發展計劃的首期工程，包括一座樓高六層的商業建築，內設百貨公司、零售商店、美食廣場、餐館、卡拉OK、保齡球場以及小型電影院等設施。

大廈呈矩形設計，前部分為購物商場，寬敞的走廊環繞著三個別具特色的中庭，中庭以一字形排列並透進天然光線，其他商業及娛樂設施則分佈於商場的後半部。

大廈的立面處理均以不同顏色的噴漆為主，加上少量裝飾，效果簡樸鮮明。而正門的鋁面雨蓬上方亦預留了大型廣告位置，簡單中顯出活力，成為該廈的獨特標誌。

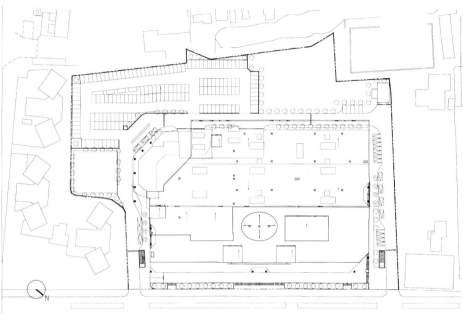

2

3

1   Perspective
2   Roof plan
3   Front facade perspective
4   Shopping arcade front elevation

1   透視圖
2   層頂平面圖
3   商場正面外觀
4   商場正立面圖

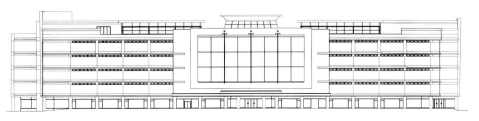

4

Dragonair/CNAC Headquarters

Design 1996
Chep Lap Kok, Hong Kong
Dragonair/CNAC
38,000 square metres
Reinforced concrete
Aluminium flat panel and glass

港龍航空 / 中國航空公司總部大樓

設計年份：1996 年
香港赤鱲角
港龍航空 / 中國航空公司
建築面積：38,000 平方米
建築材料：鋼筋混凝土、鋁平板及玻璃

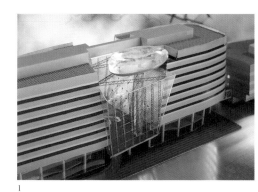

1

This is a submission for an invited competition to design a shared headquarters for two airlines at Hong Kong's new airport at Chek Lap Kok.

The prominent headland location, clearly visible from both the flight path and an adjacent highway, demanded a conspicuous design. The project comprises two fused 10-storey office blocks with communal facilities. A multi-purpose conference suite, a gymnasium, training rooms and a canteen are located in the main building. A warehouse and flight simulator rooms occupy a five-storey block linked to the main building by a glass bridge.

The challenge of creating a bicentric piece of architecture with clear corporate delineation is met by positioning a six-storey glass-roofed atrium between the two office components. On each side of the foyer, giant logos serve as clear signposts.

A bubble elevator ascends from the foyer to the aluminium-clad, airship-shaped multi-purpose conference suite located at roof level. From the air, both the transparent-roofed atrium and the conference facility articulate this important elevation.

The building form is tapered to resemble an aircraft wing when seen from a departing aircraft; horizontal bands on the elevation provide clear definition when seen from the highway.

這項設計工程除了為參加一項設計邀請賽外，亦是為兩家航空公司設計位於新機場的一座共用總部大樓。

總部大樓座落在一塊凸出的岬地上，可以從機場跑道和毗鄰的公路上見到，因此，在設計上採用了引人注目的方案。工程由兩座互相緊扣，樓高十層，配備各項公用服務設施的辦公大樓組成。在主樓內，設有一間多用途會議廳、健身室、訓練室及餐廳。一個倉庫及多間模擬飛行駕駛室，則置於由一條玻璃天橋與主樓連接的一座五層高的大樓內。

一座六層高天井，把兩座辦公大樓互相緊扣，而兩座大樓的大堂分別設有兩間公司的標誌，成功地表達出兩間公司的個別形像及合作無間的關係。

該座天井的頂層以玻璃搭建，為一個外型象飛船的多用途會議室，並由一部觀光電梯來往地下大堂至頂層，從空中俯瞰，透明的屋頂及先進的會議設施，盡顯這座重要建築物的特點。若從飛機上眺望，總部大樓的外形更尤如飛機的兩翼。從公路上遠望，圍繞大樓外牆的水平色帶便成為明顯特徵。

2

1 Model: note the airship-shaped conference room
2 Facade detail
3 Ground floor plan
4 Zoning
5 The six-storey atrium acts as an entrance to the two
  buildings
6 Long section
7 Entrance elevation

1 模型：呈太空船形狀的會議室
2 立面細部
3 地面平面圖
4 分區圖
5 6層樓高的大堂用作兩座建築物的入口
6 長剖面圖
7 入口立面圖

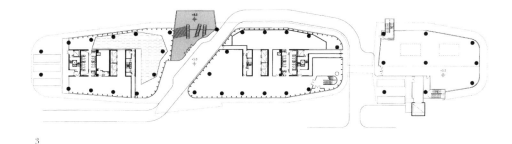

3

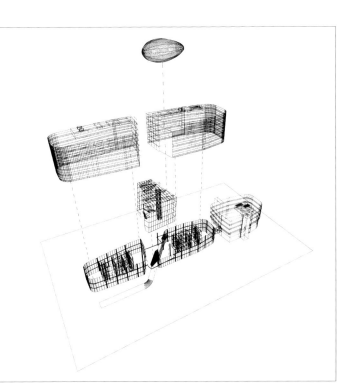

4

5

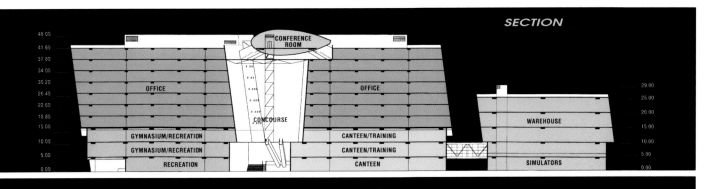

6

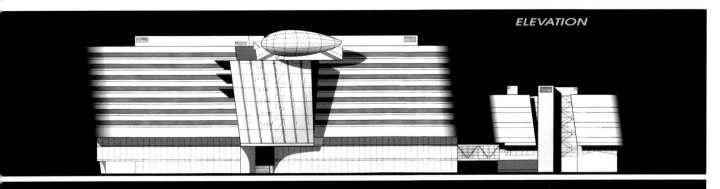

7

Island Place

Design/Completion 1992/1997
North Point, Hong Kong
Swire Properties/Island Communication
Developments Ltd
147,000 square metres (15,573 square
metres retail; 43,871 square metres office;
59,311 square metres residential)
784 residential units
Reinforced concrete
Reflective glass

港運城

設計年份／完成年份：1992 年 /1997 年
香港北角
Swire and Island Communication Developments Ltd.
建築面積：147,000 平方米 (15,573 平方米零售商場、
43,871 平方米寫字樓、59,311 平方米住宅)
784 個住宅單位
建築材料：鋼筋混凝土、反光玻璃、
顏色鋁板及麻石外牆

Substantial site and road preparation were
required in a dense urban district prior to
construction of this mixed-use development.
One 32-storey and two 33-storey residential
blocks and a 26-storey office tower are organised
linearly, anchored by a four-storey retail podium.

Orientation of the residential blocks towards a
side road avoids excessive noise pollution and
the podium itself functions as a buffer.

Patterned glass and stone ornament the
elevation. The residential and retail components
are dressed in pink, while the office wears
orange. Reflective glass panels top the
residential blocks and the office tower is
accented with decorative cathode tube lighting.
Height and space are emphasised through the
geometric truncation of the buildings' elements.

The retail portion is semi-exposed to the full-
height lobby and consists of a four-storey atrium
with an irregular glass facade for maximum
visibility at street level. The two upper floors
provide parking spaces for 288 cars.

The development is intended as inspiration for a
rewrite of this non-core area.

在動工興建這項綜合用途物業之前，需要在建築物
密集的市區，進行大量的地盤及道路準備工程。整體的
設計是一座32層和兩座33層高的住宅大廈、及一座26層
高的寫字樓大廈，以一字形排列在一座4層高的購物
商場上，商場上面兩層，則為可停泊228部私家車的
停車場。

各座住宅大廈均面向一條側面較偏僻的街道，以減低
噪音對對居民做成的滋擾，而購物商場本身亦起噪音
緩衝的作用。住宅大廈的頂部裝設反光玻璃幕牆，
寫字樓大廈頂部則採用陰極管照明系統。

住宅大廈和購物商場的外牆為粉紅色，而寫字樓大廈
以橙色為主色。建築物的正面，採用圖案玻璃和石板
裝飾，並以幾何設計加強了高度及空間的發揮。購物商
場半外露式大堂設計，使街上行人可透過不規則的
玻璃面，盡覽商場內的四層高中庭。

此項工程成了非核心區重建計劃的另一代表作。

1

2

1 Entrance lobby decorative portal
2 The complex consists of four tower blocks atop a retail podium
3 Glazed outcrops create views to the street
4 Section through east atrium
5 Plan of landscaped podium deck and office block
6 Entrance lobby of office tower
7 Street-level view of retail podium

1 辦公室大堂入口裝飾門
2 聳立於基座平台上的4幢建築物
3 面向大街的玻璃飾面商場部分
4 東西天井部分的剖面圖
5 建築物的整體平面圖
6 辦公室大廈地下大堂
7 坐落於行人路旁的商舖從行人路觀看商舖

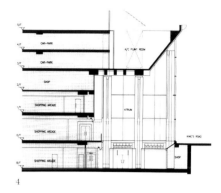

3

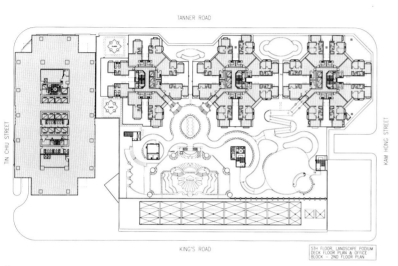

4

5

6

7

10

8

11

9

12

13

14

15

16

Hung Shui Kiu Residential Development

Design/Completion 1995/1999
Yuen Long, New Territories, Hong Kong
CITIC Pacific Ltd
49,815 square metres
Reinforced concrete post and beam structure
Tinted green glass curtain wall, black anodised
aluminium window wall, mirrored stainless
steel

洪水橋住宅發展計劃

設計年份/完成年份：1995年/1999年
香港新界元朗
中信泰富有限公司 CITIC Pacific Ltd.
建築面積：49,815平方米
建築結構：鋼筋混凝土柱樑結構
建築材料：綠色玻璃幕牆、黑色陽極化鋁窗牆、
鏡面不銹鋼、瓷磚及雲石

1

A constrained site bordered by the busy Castle
Peak Road and Tin Shui Wai West Access Road
hosts this residential development. In all,
11 towers, ranging from 11 to 17 storeys, are
organised around the periphery of this
irregularly shaped site. Due to the noisy road
system, the towers face inwards onto a
landscaped central park. A four-storey, fully
glazed clubhouse and a swimming pool occupy
the west of the site. At the site apex stands an
eight-storey car park with a rooftop tennis court.
This building also functions as a noise buffer.

All the blocks and facilities are linked by a metal
covered walkway which winds across the site. The
structurally paired blocks share an 8-metre-high
glass atrium which allows visual connection with
the park.

As the rears of the blocks address the highway,
they constitute a major elevation. The expression
of this elevation relies on exposing elements
which are normally concealed, such as the lift
lobbies and the glass-encased staircases.

The front elevations are articulated by the green-
tinted glass curtain walls of the living rooms,
which allow park views.

Of particular interest is the flexibility in the mix
of units. The walls between adjacent units are
not fixed, so two flats can be combined.
Likewise, there is flexibility between upper and
lower floors, facilitating the creation of duplexes.

這項住宅發展計劃的地盤，以交通繁忙的青山公路和
天水圍西部通路為地界。全部合共有十一幢住宅大廈，
分別由十一至十七層高，沿著該處一塊不規則形狀的
土地周邊排列。地盤的西端設有一座全玻璃外牆的
高四層會所大樓及一個游泳池。而北面則設有一座八層
高的停車場大樓，頂層更設有網球場，而這座大樓亦
具有具噪音屏障的作用。

所有住宅大廈及設施，均由一條有蓋行人道連接，
而每兩座住宅大廈會共用一個八米高的玻璃電梯大堂。
這個玻璃大堂，使住宅大廈與中央公園看起來像是連接
起來。

由於各座大廈的背後為繁忙的公路，主要的客廳均面
向中央公園，以減低鄰近高噪音的公路對住客的滋擾，
外牆更以綠色落地玻璃鋪砌，使住客能夠飽覽公園
景色。而面對公路方向的主要為受噪音影響較低的附加
設施，例如電梯大堂、逃生樓梯、廚房和洗手間等。

創意新穎的設計，讓各個相鄰的住宅單位可以靈活組
合。由於相鄰單位之間的隔牆不是固定的，因此，可以
將兩個單位合二為一，同樣，上下兩層的單位亦可
組合成複式單位。

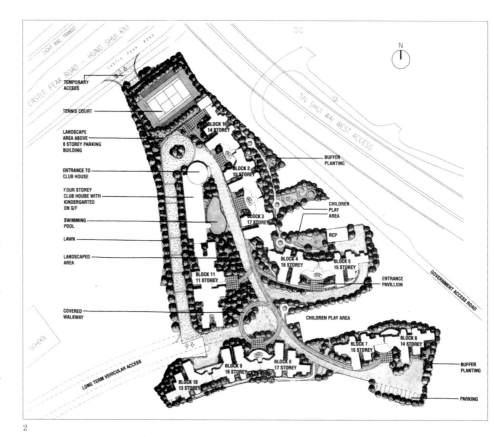

2

3

1	Elevation	1	立面圖
2	Master layout plan	2	總平面圖
3	Model	3	模型

Chek Lap Kok Telephone Exchange

Design/Completion 1994/1998
Chek Lap Kok, Hong Kong
Hong Kong Telecom/New World/Hutchison
2,460 square metres
Reinforced concrete
Glazed mosaic tiles, blue tinted reflective glass

赤鱲角電話機樓

設計年份 / 完成年份：1994 年 /1998 年
香港赤鱲角
香港電訊 / 新世界電訊 / 和記電訊
建築面積：2,460 平方米
建築結構：鋼筋混凝土、釉面銀色瓷磚、藍色玻璃

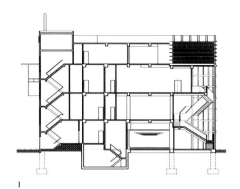

1

This four-storey building houses the telephone exchange facilities for the new airport at Chek Lap Kok. The project is designed to accommodate telecommunications equipment and will not be manned.

Located at the south-west corner of the island amongst other airport support facilities, the exchange is linked to a sophisticated local traffic network. The main cables enter the basement and are distributed to the three telephone company user groups, each of which occupies a designated compartment.

The design conforms to the specifications detailed in the airport's design guideline, ensuring that it complements adjacent buildings in both form and colour.

The high-tech elevation is concerned with the expression of function. A glass cylindrical entrance adds distinction, its transparent skin highlighting the staircase inside. To maximise accessibility, this entrance is positioned at the north-east corner of the site where it is highly visible from the main road.

Aluminium sun-shading fins and cantilevered projections trim the simple rectilinear form. The elevation is tiled in shades of silver with clear expression of seams. Streamlined fenestration reinforces the technology-driven design.

這座四層高的大樓內，安裝了新機場的電話交匯設施，而這些電訊設備是完全自動化的。

電話機樓與其它機場支援設施，均座落於大嶼山的西南方，而機樓與一個先進的本地交通網絡連接。電話總纜置於地庫，然後分配予三家電話公司的用戶，每個用戶使用一個指定的分隔間。

電話機樓的設計，必須符合機場設計指引中列明的技術規範，確保其建築格式及顏色均與毗鄰建築物相互配合。

大樓的設計，反映了建築物高科技的用途。一個玻璃的圓筒入口，使其特徵更加突出；透明的外殼，突出了入口內的樓梯設計。大樓入口面向東北方主要道路，增加大廈的人流量。

大樓外牆以釉面銀色瓷磚及藍色玻璃門窗組合出簡單的直線外型及流線形的設計，加強建築物高科技的建築特色。

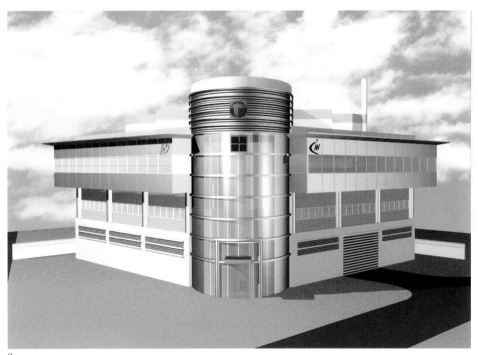

2

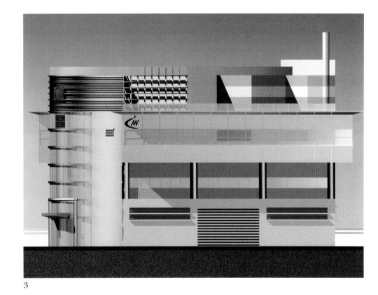

3

1 Section
2 Perspective
3 North elevation

1 剖面圖
2 透視圖
3 北立面圖

Nationwealth Plaza

Design/Completion 1995/1997
Beijing, China
Tai Yu International Investment Group Ltd
221,400 square metres
Reinforced concrete
Granite, curtain wall, aluminium panels

北京富國廣場

設計年份/完成年份：1995 年/1997 年
中國北京
台友國際投資集團有限公司
建築面積：221,400 平方米
建築材料：花崗岩石、幕牆、鋁板

This multi-use project comprises three office towers ranging from 12 to 29 storeys and a 26-storey residential block atop a six-storey podium.

The retail podium houses a commercial complex containing a retail arcade, a bowling alley, restaurants, a food court, a cinema, department stores and a private clubhouse. Each activity is organised in fluid zones and is linked by strategic vertical transportation systems. The centre of the retail podium features a vast cone-shaped void which is the focal point of the arcade.

The towers are located on the podium perimeter, allowing much of the roof to be used as a landscaped deck. Differences in tower height and massing create a visual rhythm which climaxes with a cascading antenna crown on the largest office block. The office plans vary from curvilinear, through rectilinear, to a sculpted "elbow" design, while the residential block adopts a cruciform plan.

The surface treatment of the complex—an ensemble of rich granite and curtain wall banded with aluminium panels—is sleek and modern.

這座多功能的綜合性建築項目，是由6層高的裙樓、三座12至29層高的辦公塔樓及一座26層高的住宅大廈所組成。

商場設於裙樓之中，內有百貨公司、零售商店、保齡球場、電影院、美食廣場、餐館及一個私人會所。裙樓的中央部份是一個圓錐形的中庭，不同活動區域分佈其中，由樓層內各組升降機互相連接。

各座塔樓分佈在裙樓的四周位置，其高度不一，疏密有緻，形成一種高低起伏的視覺效果。寫字樓備有多個不同的間隔設計，以切合個別用途，而住宅則採用十字形的佈局設計。

高層住宅平面呈方形，每層8戶，二室戶和三室戶各佔一半，最高兩層則為複式單位。大廈的外牆以名貴的花崗石、鋁板及玻璃幕牆作飾面。

1

2

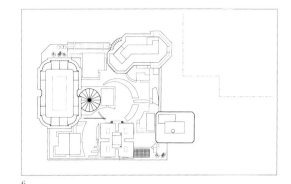

6

3

7

4

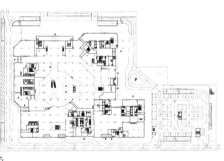

5

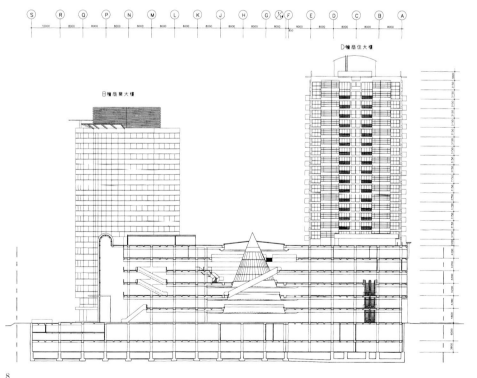

8

CRC Development

Design/Completion 1992/1994
Cheung Sha Wan, West Kowloon, Hong Kong
China Resource Company/Yuen Fat Wharf &
Godown Company
10,431 square metres (3,759 square metres
administration building; 466 square metres
maintenance building; 3,094 square metres
cargo shed; 3,112 square metres transit shed)
Reinforced concrete
Aluminium cladding

This project is a cargo trans-shipment complex
providing berthing and cargo handling by land
and sea at a newly reclaimed waterfront location.
The complex comprises a seven-storey
administration building, two cargo storage
stations, a maintenance building and other
ancillary facilities.

The building's architectural treatment reflects its
industrial character, which is manifested in the
mechanical penthouse, metal cladding,
geometric framing and organisation of the roof
trusses.

A recessed top floor in the administration
building is home to an executive suite and also
gives access to the rooftop observation platform
which surveys the entire site. To maintain the
rhythm of the complex, the roof design of the
cargo stations is derived from a structural bay,
giving rise to a series of north-facing celestial
windows which flood the interior with light.

新華潤發倉庫碼頭發展工程

設計年份 / 完成年份：1992 年 /1994 年
香港西九龍長沙灣
華潤有限公司 / 潤發倉碼有限公司
建築面積：10,431 平方米 (3,759 平方米行政樓、
466 平方米維修樓、3,094 平方米貨倉、
3,112 平方米轉口倉)
建築材料：鋼筋混凝土、鋁質覆面

該建築工程項目是一個位於西九龍填海區的綜合貨櫃轉
口設施，提供海、陸兩方面的貨櫃轉運及停泊服務。
設施包括一座七層高的行政大樓、兩座貨倉、一座維修
船塢、碼頭及其他的輔助設施。

整個建築物的選料及顏色配襯皆能表現出其本身的工業
特性，例如採用金屬及幾何圖形的構件等。行政大樓
外牆鋪以淺色反光玻璃幕牆及銀色鋁面，其頂層面積比
其他樓層略減，用作高級行政人員的辦公室，並可經
由此層直達樓頂的瞭望平台，鳥瞰整個倉庫的全景。

為了保持整體設計的特色，兩座單層貨倉表面亦採用了
銀色鋁質覆面，並使用紅藍兩色作為門、窗顏色的基
調，以增加其顯著性。而貨倉的頂部更設有多排斜向的
天窗，令引入的天然光線，與鋼樑的結構，形成一個
強烈的對比。

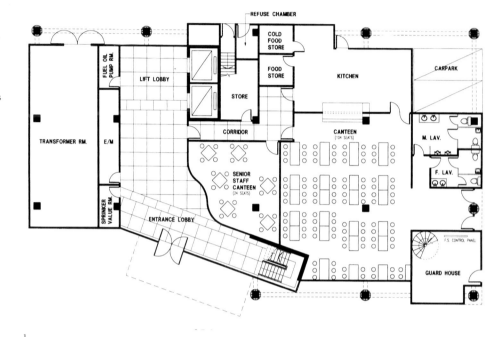

1

2

1 Ground floor plan
2 Metal-clad storage sheds with north-facing roof lights
3 Aerial view of the complex
4 The seven-storey administration block clad in metal
   and glass

1 地面平面圖
2 金屬板覆面倉庫配以向北層頂射燈
3 高空鳥瞰
4 金屬板及玻璃飾面的7層高行政大樓

3

4

5

6

7

8

9

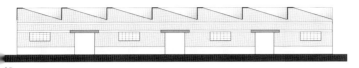

10

13

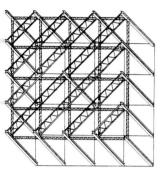
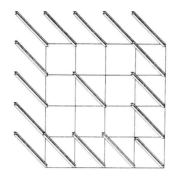

11

14

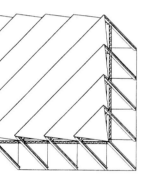
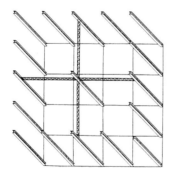

12

12

15

Nanjing Tong Lu Commercial Development

Design/Completion 1995/1999
Shanghai, China
Henderson (China) Investment Co. Ltd
36,395 square metres
Reinforced concrete
Glass, granite

上海大三元商業發展計劃

設計年份 / 完成年份：1995 年 /1999 年
中國上海
建築面積；36,395 平方米
建築材料：鋼筋混凝土、玻璃、花崗岩石

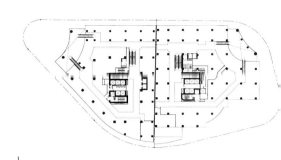

1

The project, situated on a triangular site fronting Nanjing Tong Lu Road, consists of a five-storey retail podium with a 22-storey office tower above. In responding to the characteristics of the site, the development—with its set-back tower—addresses the main road, reinforcing the existing medium-rise urban edge. An urban landscaped plaza is established at the tip of the site, fronting the main entrance of the retail podium, and this signals a welcome to passers-by.

The grandeur of the main entrance is emphasised with a five-storey void crowned with a turret. Inside, retail activity is focused around this arcade void.

The facade treatment employs a classical system and order while using modern details, thus creating a refreshing style that is contemporary yet respectful of its context.

The tower, with its curvilinear frontage, maximises its exposure along the main facade while at the same time softening the apex of the triangular site, generating an asymmetrical composition. This, together with the curved main entrance below, expresses the dynamic nature of the locale.

這幢商業大廈位處上海市中心南京東路的繁盛商業區，
由5層高的商業裙樓及22層高的辦公塔樓所組成。
地盤西端的南京東路及湖北路轉角地段闢有一個佔地
500平方米的綠化廣場，作為建築物的正門前的人流集
散地及休憩處，這部分一直延伸至4層高的入口中庭大
堂。

辦公塔樓的正面呈弧形，以取得最廣闊的視野，並避免
遮擋隔鄰的商廈。由於其特殊的地理位置，建築設計必
須配合四周的環境，並盡量與鄰近已列為受保護的
建築物作呼應，而又不失現代商業建築的特色。故此，
在立面處理上，乃揉合古典的裝飾與現代建築的技術，
配以新型的建築材料，使大廈與周圍的環境相互協調。

2

3

1 Typical floor plan
2 Perspective
3 Elevation

1 標準層平面圖
2 透視圖
3 立面圖

Post-graduate Hostel at the Chinese University of Hong Kong

Design/Completion 1996/1998
Shatin, New Territories, Hong Kong
Chinese University of Hong Kong
13,425 square metres
Reinforced concrete
Ceramic tiles, aluminium windows

香港中文大學研究生宿舍

設計年份／完成年份：1996 年／1998 年
香港新界沙田
香港中文大學
建築面積：13,425 平方米
建築材料：鋼筋混凝土、瓷磚、鋁窗

1

This hostel comprises student accommodation, a multi-purpose hall, function rooms, a warden's apartment and support facilities. The project is situated at the base of a mountain overlooking Tolo Harbour and, closer to home, the university's stadium. The planning and design are much influenced by the rural location.

The cascading arrangement of the five blocks is modelled on the contours of the mountainous backdrop on one side, while the other side addresses the axis of the stadium. The design is such that each elevation constitutes a major face of the building. The blocks, composed of modules, are interlocking and follow a curvilinear, L-shaped outline. Each module has 10 bedrooms and wash facilities on each floor and is linked to its neighbour by a system of nodes which contain pantries, sitting rooms and the circulation network.

The entrance lobby is housed in a node with more exaggerated dimensions than the rest and with a feature roof. The hostel is accessed from the front by a landscaped terrace which climbs into the raised body of the building. At the rear, an elevated covered walkway feeds into this primary node. Additional site landscaping articulates the nature-oriented design concept.

該宿舍大樓座落於山腳位置，遠眺吐露港，靠近大學運動場。大樓內除設有學生宿舍外，尚有一個多用途的禮堂、多間活動室、一間舍監宿舍，及其他支援設施。

宿舍的規劃乃盡量配合其所處的地理環境，建築物依山而建，其平面呈Y型，三個方向的交匯點是一座圓筒形的主樓，內置主入口大廳及升降機，作為整座宿舍縱橫方向的中心點。

宿舍分為三座，各座相連並作弧形及直角排列。每座的標準層分設有10間寢室及一盥洗間，中間通道的兩旁為備餐間及客廳，而舍監宿舍則位於頂層部分。

主樓的正門入口處為一片扇形的綠化平台，並以此中心向外伸展；另外還可通過一條有蓋的行人道進入建築物內。建築物的整體設計與四周的翠綠環境互相配合，並巧妙地與大自然景緻融為一體。

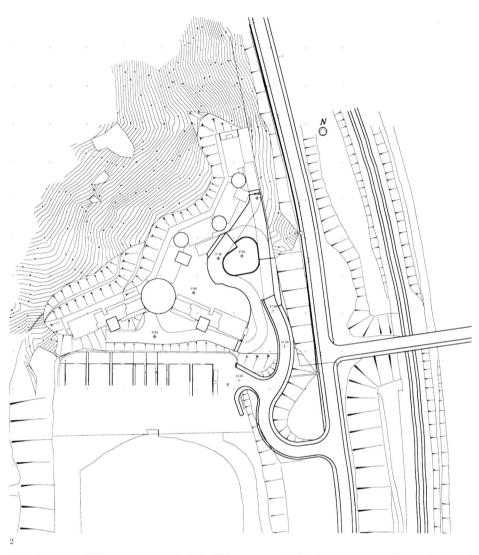

2

1   Interior perspective
2   Site plan
3   Perspective

1   室內透視圖
2   位置圖
3   透視圖

3

Discovery Bay North Master Plan

Design/Completion 1996/2004
Lantau Island, Hong Kong
Hong Kong Resort Company Ltd
979,345 square metres
Reinforced concrete structure with stone
cladding, ceramic tiles, aluminium windows

愉景灣北部擴展計劃

設計年份 / 完成年份：1996 年 /2004 年
香港大嶼山
Hong Kong Resort Company Ltd.
建築面積：979,345 平方米
建築材料：鋼筋混凝土結構外牆配石板、
瓷磚、鋁窗

This natural extension to the existing Discovery Bay development extends over 53.5 hectares of virgin land on Lantau Island, which is to undergo extensive reclamation and site formation.

The scope of the planning includes 210,000 square metres of high-, mid- and low-rise residential development supported by a shopping mall, a hotel and comprehensive community amenities, including two international schools.

In addition, there are plans for extensive civil works, including a new pier, bus station and tunnel to Shiu Ho Wan, which will eventually link up to the North Lantau Expressway and the new airport at Chek Lap Kok. This tunnel will route service vehicles and shuttle buses to and from the site, marking a new era for the previously cloistered Discovery Bay.

The residential portion is to be erected in phases, although the development has been planned as a whole so that a cohesive identity is assured. Due to the variety of residential forms and the requirement for sea views, the high-rise blocks fan the rear of the site with the low-rise developments organised on stepped platforms leading down to the shoreline.

This new generation of residences is grouped in 24-storey high-rises, six-storey low-rises and two-storey townhouses. As in the original Discovery Bay development, open space and landscaping are prioritised. A key component of the scheme is a park which segregates the new development from its predecessor. The high-rise towers adopt a slab block design with only six units per floor. An elongated scheme allows sea views from all of the units, even from kitchens and bathrooms.

愉景灣北部發展計劃佔地53.5公頃，位於大嶼山一帶由填海及平整工程而得來的土地。發展範圍包括總建築面積達210,000平方米的高層、中層及低層住宅樓宇，附設購物商場、酒店、康樂及綜合社區服務設施以及兩所國際學校。而擴建計劃的其中一部分是在新發展區與原來的發展區之間興建一個中央公園。

此外，計劃中還有多項土木工程項目，包括一個新碼頭、巴士總站，以及一條通往小蠔灣並連接北大嶼山快速公路與赤鱲角新機場的隧道，作為該新發展區的主要輔助交通系統。

該發展項目的整體規劃已經完成，住宅部分將會分期興建。這些新建的住宅樓宇，樓高分別為6層和24層，另有兩層高的平房。按原本的發展計劃，園林及露天休憩場地均為精心處理，而其他建築設計亦與別不同。而為了令所有住宅樓宇有更佳景觀，高層大廈將坐落於土地的後面部分，而低層樓宇會逐級排列，一直伸延至岸邊。大廈每樓層只有6個住宅單位，並作長形方式設計，使各單位均能享有海景。同時，單位的室內佈置亦非常講究，以確保住戶有舒適的環境。

1

2

3

4

5

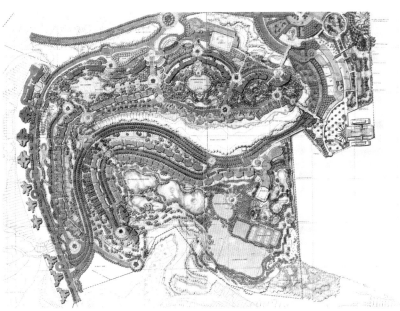

6

Pristine Villa

Design/Completion 1988/1994
Tao Fung Shan, Shatin, New Territories,
Hong Kong
Newfid Co. Ltd
52,800 square metres (498 residential units)
Reinforced concrete wall
Ceramic mosaic tiles

曉翠山莊

設計年份/完成年份：1988 年/1994 年
香港新界道風山
建築面積：52,800 平方米(498 住宅單位)
建築結構：鋼筋混凝土牆
建築材料：彩色瓷磚

Located on a 44,592-square metre site in private
parkland, this project comprises 498 units
housed in 14 blocks of eight to ten storeys;
a four-storey car park accommodating 747 cars;
and a two-storey clubhouse with lounge,
gymnasium, squash and tennis courts,
snooker room, sauna and swimming pool.
The development occupies only 9 per cent of
this wooded site.

The housing blocks are low-rise so as not
to obstruct sight lines to the mountains.
In organisation and massing, the architecture
observes the valley's contours. The blocks are
equally divided into two groups which rise
from curvilinear podiums.

A "modern Romantic" theme dominates the
design and is expressed through the soft pink,
tile-clad facades banded in orange and green on
lower floors. The scheme is further enlivened by
the orange, glazed floating walls which articulate
the end blocks in each group.

Inside, primary spaces are oriented to views of
the park, where recreation opportunities include
an adventure playground and barbecue area.

1

曉翠山莊座落於私人公園內一塊面積44,592平方米的
土地上，由十四座四層高、合共498個住宅單位的住宅
樓宇；一座四層樓高，設有747個私家車位的停車場；
以及一座兩層高，設有休息室、健身室、壁球室、
網球場、桌球室、桑拿浴室及游泳池的會所大樓組成。
在這塊林木茂盛的 土地上，建築物佔地面積僅為9%。

各座住宅均為低層樓宇，因此不會妨礙四周群山景緻。
建築師在細心觀察過山谷的地形，才組織建築物配置，
使各座樓宇平均分為兩組，建立在波浪形的平台上。

山莊以 現代羅曼蒂克為主題設計。低層顏色為柔和的
粉紅色、橙色及綠色，以條型瓷磚蓋面，其餘各層則
採用橙色釉面浮牆，使建築物外型更加生動活潑。

樓宇內的各主要房間均能飽覽公園景色，而公園內則
設有一個歷奇樂園和一個燒烤區。

1   Blocks are of different heights to reduce the "wall"
    effect
2   Blocks are clad with pink tiles banded in orange
    and green at lower levels
3   The clubhouse
4   Lift lobby of clubhouse
5   Karaoke room
6   A well-equipped gymnasium
7   Entrance lobby
8   Clubhouse facade detail
9   Aerial view of clubhouse, pool and tennis courts
10 Ceiling of clubhouse foyer

1   高低有序的建築物看來不致太單調
2   建築物舖以粉紅色瓷磚並在低層部分加上橙色及綠色的飾帶
3   會所
4   會所電梯大堂
5   卡拉OK房
6   健身室
7   住宅大堂入口
8   會所正面細部
9   從高處俯瞰會所泳池及網球場
10 會所天花設計

2

7

8

3

9

4

5

6

10

Chung On Terrace

Design/Completion 1996/1999
North Point, Hong Kong
Sun Hung Kai Properties
36,295 square metres
Reinforced concrete
Granite, granite-mix ceramic tiles, aluminium
windows

中安台

設計年份/完成年份：1996年/1999年
地點：香港北角
發展商：新鴻基地產
建築面積：36,295平方米
建築材料：鋼筋混凝土、花崗岩石、瓷、鋁窗

This project is a residential development occupying a secluded site behind King's Road. It comprises 464 units, a car park, a two-level clubhouse, a swimming pool and deck with play area, and a tennis court. The units are distributed over two back-to-back tripartite blocks, each 50 storeys high, elevated on a fortress-like podium. The resulting faceting of the facades establishes extensive views from the units. This reworking of the medieval fortress design—an allusion to the nearby Fortress Hill—is used to convey a sense of exclusivity and security.

The driveway cuts through lush greenery to an entrance courtyard framed by water features which extend across the sculpted podium facia, recalling a moat. A hanging bridge, stonework and narrow windows offer further pseudo-fortification. The clubhouse is displayed above the podium—inviolable yet conspicuous.

The rectilinear elevations of the towers are crowned with sculptures which will be lit by night. The residential layout is unusual in that it accommodates a complex unit mix. Larger units occupy the higher floors with views out over the harbour to the mountainscape behind.

位於炮台山道的一項住宅物業，由兩座背向的50層高
建築物所組成，內設有390個住宅單位、停車場、
住客會所、私人游泳池、遊樂場施設及網球場等。
建築物矗立在一個堡疊似的墩座平台上，由三部份組
成的住宅大樓令各單位均能擁有最佳的景觀。其中古堡
疊般的外型設計，亦予人一種安全及穩固的感覺。

建築物的車輛進出正門是一個以水景及雕刻裝飾所佈置
而成的庭院，這些裝飾一直伸延至墩座平台部份，
而住客會所則設於這平台上，那些吊橋、石雕及窗花
設計更進一步營造出仿古城堡的特色。

大廈的直線形立面上均裝有在夜間會發光的雕刻裝飾。
複式及較大的單位設於大廈的高層，可盡覽海港景緻。

1   Two blocks above the fortress-like podium
2   The styling of the podium alludes to nearby
    Fortress Hill
3   Bird's-eye view

1   兩幢住宅大樓聳立於堡疊狀的平台上
2   基座平台獨特的設計令人聯想到鄰近的炮台山
3   鳥瞰圖

1

2

3

Yunnan Lane LDC Development

Design/Completion 1996/2001
Yaumatei, Kowloon, Hong Kong
Land Development Corporation
39,462 square metres
Reinforced concrete
Aluminium panels, glass curtain wall

土地發展公司雲南里綜合重建計劃

設計年份/完成年份：1995 年/2001 年
香港九龍雲南里
土地發展公司
建築面積：39,462 平方米
建築材料：鋼筋混凝土、鋁板材、玻璃幕牆

This 35-storey commercial development is part of an urban renewal programme through which run-down districts are redeveloped with the proviso that restitution is made in the form of civic facilities. In this case, a public toilet, refuse collection point, day nursery, street sleeper shelter and day relief centre have been included in the scheme.

New open space fronts the office block and is linked visually and physically to the tower's second floor entrance lobby by a staircase and escalator. The landscaped space includes trees and a feature wall which reduce the impact of the adjacent built environment. This green space also provides an alternative thoroughfare for pedestrians, reducing foot traffic loads in a busy district.

The two-storey podium houses retail outlets and GIC (Government/Institution/Community) facilities. The podium and tower are designed as interlocking elements, thus breaking down the massive scale and integrating the development with the existing mid-rise fabric.

The glass-encased lobby stands in the centre of the exposed podium roof, which is bordered by columns. This elevational hiatus suggests that the tower is floating. The transparent lobby enclosure allows a subtle transition between public and private space.

Horizontal bands wrap the elevation, enabling identification from a distance. A rooftop antenna, aligned with the vista from Temple Street, adds further distinction.

這座35層高的商業大廈，是市區重建計劃的其中一部份。根據市區重建計劃，舊區重建時，附帶條件是必須重新配置各種市政設施。因此，在發展計劃中，將包括建設公眾休憩花園公廁、垃圾收集站、日間護理院、露宿者庇護所、以及日間護理中心。

辦公室大樓前面新設的露天場地，經由一道樓梯及電動扶梯，與大廈二樓入口大堂，產生視覺上及實際的連接。景觀區種植有樹木，並加建了一幅甚具特色的牆壁，以減少噪音對毗鄰樓宇住客做成的滋擾。這塊綠化空地亦新闢了一條行人通道，以舒緩繁忙區域的人流負荷。

兩層高的低座平台內，設有零售商店、各種政府及社區設施。低座平台和大廈設計高低相接並相輔相成，使密集比例降低，並且使其與現有的中等高度樓宇群和諧結合。

外露的平台中央，設有一座玻璃覆蓋大堂，並以多根柱圍繞。這種立面設計，使大廈有如浮在水面上，亦令公眾地方與私家地方之間出現微妙的過度。

大廈外牆包圍著多道水平飾帶，頂部更豎立一支獨立天線面向廟街，使大廈更具特色，而遊人從遠處亦能輕易地辨認。

1   Main elevation, view from Temple Street

1   面向廟街的建築物外貌

1

Fung Shing Street Residential Development

Design/Completion 1995/1999
Ngau Chi Wan, Kowloon, Hong Kong
Sun Hung Kai Properties
65,400 square metres
Reinforced concrete
Granite, ceramic tiles, glass, curtain wall

豐盛街住宅發展計劃

設計年份/完成年份：1995 年/1999 年
香港九龍牛池灣
新鴻基地產發展有限公司
建築面積：65,400 平方米
建築材料：鋼筋混凝土、花崗石、瓷磚、顏色玻璃

1

The site of this residential development is steeply sloped to the north and enjoys panoramic views of the harbour and Hong Kong Island to the south. The block layout reflects the need to exploit views, light and space while ensuring maximum development potential.

The four towers stand on a three-storey podium which houses a clubhouse and car park and is topped with a landscaped roof garden. The towers are linked by a continuous walkway which runs one level above the podium garden. After entering a grand, naturally lit, double-volume entrance foyer at ground level, residents can ascend to the covered walkway and enjoy views onto the garden, swimming pool and children's play areas on their way to the lift lobbies for each tower.

A heightened sense of scale lessens the visual impact of the tight massing. Homogeneity is the key to the elevational expression; a continuous sun-shading screen with varying heights of three, six and ten storeys wraps itself around the towers, resulting in a strong horizontal rhythm. This feature, together with the curtain wall at the top three storeys and horizontal caps at roof level, gives the development a unique identity.

該項住宅發展計劃的地盤、北面依傍陡坡，南面儘覽海港和香港島美景。樓宇的佈局設計，在確保最佳發展潛力的前提下，反映出對風景、光線和空間的需要。

四座住宅大廈，座落在一座三層高的裙樓上。裙樓內設有一所會所和一個停車場，頂部則設有一個景觀化平台花園。各座住宅大廈，由平台花園上方的一道行人天橋連接著。設在地面層的華麗入口大廳引入大量的天然光線，住客可經由有蓋行人天橋抵達各座大廈的電梯大堂，途中更可觀賞平台花園、游泳池以及兒童遊樂場的不同景色。

建築物在比例上突顯一種高聳的感覺，舒緩了樓宇之間緊迫的視覺影響。建築立面設計，著重統一協調的表現手法，但頂層、中層及底層則各有變化，加添趣味。而外牆的顏色，以鮮明的配襯為主，配合最上面三層樓的落地玻璃窗和屋頂的水平蓋帽，更賦予該住宅物業眾不同的特徵。

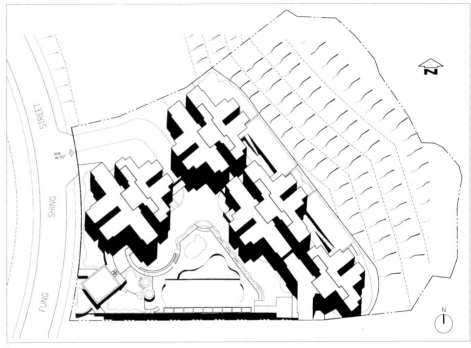

2

3

1 Elevation detail
2 Block plan
3 Landscaped podium

1 立面細部
2 總平面圖
3 平台花園

Salisbury Garden/Palace Mall

Design/Completion 1989/1996
Tsim Sha Tsui, Kowloon, Hong Kong
New World Development
13,140 square metres
Reinforced concrete, glass
Aluminium cladding, granite

梳士巴利花園及名城店

設計年份/完成年份：1989年/1996年
地點：香港九龍尖沙咀
發展商：新世界發展
建築面積：13,140平方米
建築材料：鋼筋混凝土、玻璃、鋁質覆面、花崗岩石

This project, Hong Kong's first underground shopping mall, consists of four basement levels located beneath a grand glasshouse structure. The glasshouse is integrated with the landscaped Salisbury Garden open space adjacent to the Cultural Centre and serves as a forecourt to this monumental building. The curvilinear roof and transparent anatomy of the glass structure ensure its landmark status.

The retail component at basement levels one and two is reached by an escalator system from inside the glass volume. The transparent atrium allows maximum levels of natural light to penetrate the mall. Beneath the retail levels is a two-storey, 250-space car park which is accessed via the neighbouring New World Centre car park, obviating the need for a ramp. This car park is designated for the use of Cultural Centre patrons.

Pedestrian subways connect the mall to the New World Centre, the Peninsula Hotel and the Sheraton Hotel, anticipating the time when pedestrian crossings at grade will no longer be possible in this busy area of Tsim Sha Tsui.

這座建築物是香港首座地庫購物商場，分別由四層組成。上面以透明水晶建築與景觀優美的梳士巴利公園廣場連為一體，毗鄰是香港文化中心，成了該建築物的前院。弧形屋頂和透明結構，更顯示了出色的建築設計水平。

通往地庫一層及二層的電動扶梯設於透明玻璃建築中，商場透明的建築材料讓大量陽光進入。商場下面是設有250個私家車位的雙層停車場，連接著相鄰的新世界中心的停車場，無須另建斜坡供汽車使用。此停車場更可供到訪文化中心的人士使用。

此名店城在尖沙咀這繁忙地帶，以後再沒有地面斑馬線，行人通道改向地下發展。多條行人隧道，由名店城通往新世界中心、半島酒店及喜來登酒店，構成一個新的地下行人輪紐，有助疏導路面上擠擁的人流。

1

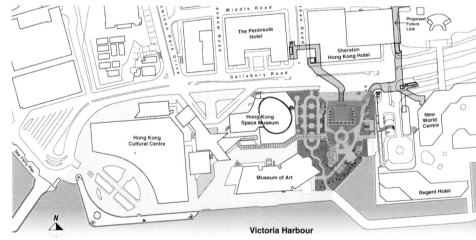

2

4

5

3

6

7

10

8

11

9

12

Haven of Hope Nursing Home Development

Design/Completion 1993/1998
Haven of Hope Hospital, Tseung Kwan O,
New Territories, Hong Kong
Haven of Hope Christian Service
7,880 square metres
Reinforced concrete column and beam
Ceramic mosaic tiles

靈實護理安老院

設計年份／完成年份：1993/1998 年
香港新界將軍澳靈實醫院
基督教靈實協會(Haven of Hope Christian Service)
建築面積：7,880 平方米
建築材料：鋼筋混凝土柱樑、彩色瓷磚

1

Located on the western slope of the hospital compound, this project bridges the gap between an infirmary and a care and attention home. Some 250 elderly people are accommodated in the seven-storey facility.

A key challenge met by the design was to replace the formality of the institution with a more domestic environment. This has been achieved by introducing natural materials such as timber and stone to the interior and using a warm palette throughout the building. Each floor has a distinctive colour scheme, which not only aids orientation but also creates a sense of identity. Communal activity areas are positioned outside dormitories to encourage interaction.

Outside, there is a podium-level Chinese garden. Planters, brises soleils and air-conditioning hoods articulate the facade, and the fenestration is organised into various configurations. To complement the scale and massing of the hospital, the linearity and massing of the building is broken into three sections by a brick coloured feature wall in the centre of the elevation. The colour scheme and materials also recall the hospital.

靈實護理安老院座落於靈實醫院西面的山坡上，大樓樓高八層，為250名六十五歲或以上的老人提供療養院及高度照顧安老院之醫療服務。

作為老人家安渡餘年的地方，該院之設計意念是以一溫暖的家居形式代替一般醫療機構予人冰冷呆板的感覺。因此，醫院內廣泛地使用溫和的色調及天然物料(包括木材及石料)。而安老院每層均預留寬敞的共用活動空間給老人家聊天及起居。

院外更建有一個中式平台花園。各種花槽、遮陽板、以及空調通氣罩，使其外形面更具生氣。為了配合醫院的比例及結構佈局，安老院的曲線外形及結構由中間的一道彩色磚牆一分為三。而所採用的色調及建築材料，亦令人聯想起靈實醫院。

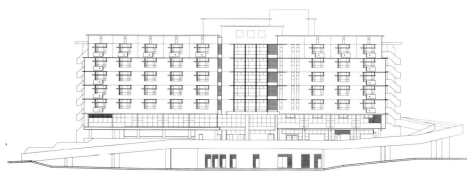

2

3

4

1   Interior perspective
2   Front elevation
3   Computer rendering of entrance
4   Perspective

1   空內透視圖
2   正立面圖
3   主要入口
4   透視圖

Park Theatre

Design/Completion 1996/1999
Tung Lo Wan Road, Causeway Bay, Hong Kong
Southland Co. Ltd
10,450 square metres
Reinforced concrete column and beam
Ceramic tiles, aluminium window wall,
aluminium cladding, glass cladding

百樂戲院重建工程

設計年份/完成年份：1996年/1999年
香港銅鑼灣銅鑼灣道
南源有限公司
建築面積：10,450平方米
建築結構：鋼筋混凝土柱樑結構
建築材料：鋁牆板、玻璃幕牆

1

Sited at the intersection of Tin Hau Temple
Street and the Tung Lo Wan Road, and
addressing the landscaped greenery of Victoria
Park, this project comprises a 19-storey office
tower positioned atop a retail podium.

To contrast with the surrounding and dated mid-
rise residential environment, the solution called
for simple, modern architectural expression,
ensuring a strong identity for the building. The
elevation is wrapped in a glass and aluminium
cladding and glass window wall system. The
glazed area is maximised so that the building
appears transparent, lightweight and clean in
contrast with the cluttered neighbourhood.

The entrance lobby to the office tower is located
on the first floor, releasing more space at the
ground floor retail level. A semi-enclosed atrium
is organised around a circular skylight which
suffuses the interior with natural light. The
banks of escalators which link the three retail
levels are exposed to the exterior, introducing a
sense of dynamism to the elevation. The external
wall of the top two podium floors is tapered to
produce variation in the building form.

該工程項目位於天后廟道及銅鑼灣道交界，面向維多
利亞公園，是一幢立於裙樓上的19層高商業大廈。

為了令該建築物比鄰近舊有的住宅樓宇更為突出，
設計以簡潔而富現代化的格調為主，突顯大廈的鮮明
形象。在立面處理上，特別採用了玻璃幕牆及鋁面
建材，其寬闊的玻璃表面，使大廈外型變得晶瑩雅緻，
與毗鄰的舊式樓宇形成一個強烈的對比。

辦公室大樓的正門入口大堂設於二樓，以便騰出更多
空間作地下零售商場。裙樓內的半開放式中庭圍繞著
一個半圓形天窗，為室內引入天然光線。從室外更可看
到用以往來三層零售商場的自動扶梯，倍添活力動感。
此外，裙樓最頂兩層的外牆成弧形狀，使建築物的
外型更見靈活多變。

1　Model
2　Perspective

1　模型
2　透視圖

2

The University of Hong Kong New Medical Complex

Design/Completion 1996/2001
Sassoon Road, Hong Kong
The University of Hong Kong
50,000 square metres
Reinforced concrete
Ceramic tiles, curtain wall, aluminium windows

香港大學新醫學院綜合大樓

設計年份 / 落成年份：1996 年 /2001 年
香港薄扶林沙宣道
香港大學
建築面積：50,000 平方米
建築材料：鋼筋混凝土、瓷磚外牆、玻璃幕牆、鋁窗

This project involves the development of a new complex for the Pre-clinical School, with the addition of a new Clinical Research Centre.

The scheme divides the facility into two zones of accommodation, separating laboratory space from non-laboratory space. The four-storey Clinical Research Centre is an extension of the Pre-clinical School.

Building heights and floor plates are designed to minimise the vertical transportation of large student groups. Emergency exit routes and associated cores are positioned on the periphery to maximise uninterrupted floor area. Three main zones of pedestrian circulation and three entrances promote smooth circulation.

The Laboratory Building is a rectangular shape based on a 1.5 x 1.5 metre planning grid which is reflected in the structural frame and window frames. This grid allows modular planning which, in turn, provides layout flexibility. Each laboratory-based department is served by an independent building services branch which can be isolated from the central system if necessary.

The Non-laboratory Building houses the Medical Education Unit, the medical library, the Teaching/Convention Centre and non-laboratory-based departments. The building's curved form maximises views out of the site and has facilitated the construction of a central, semi-circular garden within the built environment. The plan area reduces progressively on the upper floors, resulting in a stepped profile which allows sunlight into the garden.

The landscape strategy integrates existing topography with a pedestrian system including rotunda and covered walkways.

此項工程包括興建一座全新的醫科實驗室大樓，並附設一所嶄新的醫學研究中心，及教學大樓。

實驗室院大樓設有用作教學的多種學科實驗室、生物醫學研究實驗室及傳統中國醫學中心。其它設施包括醫學圖書館、演講廳、研討/導修室及職員休憩室則設於教學大樓。

大樓的高度及樓面設計，主要針對減低大群學生上落各層間的人潮。緊急通道置於大樓的外圍部份，以擴展大樓樓層實用面積。建築設計並包括三條主要行人通道和入口，讓大樓暢通無阻。

實驗室大樓的外牆用料為鋁窗及瓷磚，大樓設計以1.5米為基本組合模式，應用於長方形的外框結構，使建築物設計更具靈活性。而每個實驗室部門均有獨立的屋宇設備，緊急情況下不受中央控制。

至於教學大樓則包括了醫學教育組、醫學圖書館、教學/會議中心及非實驗室為主的部門。樓宇弧形的設計能令人盡覽室外景緻，更可配合在樓宇範圍內興建一個半圓形的中央花園。樓宇面積逐層向上遞減，形成梯級式的獨特外形，讓陽光可普照在花園中。

園景設計把現有的地形與通道系統，以及行人道結合為一個整體。

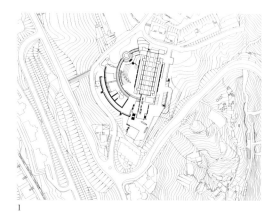

1

2

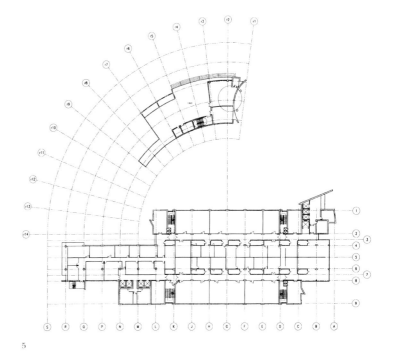

5

3

4

6

7

Tai Po Hospital

Design/Completion 1988/1997
Tai Po, New Territories, Hong Kong
Architectural Services Department
39,000 square metres
Reinforced concrete post and beam structure
Ceramic mosaic tiles

大埔醫院

設計年份 / 完成年份：1988 年 /1997 年
香港新界大埔
建築署
建築面積：39,000 平方米
建築結構：鋼筋混凝土柱樑結構
建築材料：白色瓷磚

1

Set in landscaped grounds, this six-storey complex accommodates 1,020 convalescent and infirmary beds; occupational therapy, physiotherapy, pharmacy and radiology departments; general administration units; and centralised kitchen facilities.

Functional planning is the key to the design. The hospital comprises four wings grouped around a central core in a cruciform arrangement, reflecting the need for efficiency. Wards are generally located on upper floor levels with views of the landscaped exterior. This nucleus-derived scheme adopts a streamlined vertical circulation system in both the core and the tips of the wings.

The treatment of light entering the wards is central to the elevational design. White-tiled concrete fins have been angled to reflect diffused sunlight into the building. These sun-shading devices also articulate the simple facade.

The core, which is interpreted as the trunk of the building, is further embellished with a glass block feature and capped roof. To break down the scale, the tips of the four wings are recessed and semi-circular holes are punched through the capped roofs.

Outside, a tinted, transparent covered walkway leads through landscaped grounds to the entrance courtyard where a multi-grid skylit canopy echoes the curvilinear movement of the landscape.

該座六層高的綜合性樓宇座落在一個綠化園景上，共擁有1,020個復康療養床位，並設有職業治療科、物理治療科及放射治療科等醫院輔助服務。而其他設施則有藥房、一般行政辦公室，以及集中的廚房設施。

醫院的設計，主要是按功能而作規劃。醫院以中央為核心，另外四座側翼以十字形排列，圍繞中心而建，反映效率的重要性。病房一般設在較高的樓層，讓病人能觀賞到室外的景色。而醫院的上落人潮亦帶到醫院的中心部份及各側翼的末端，使整座建築物體現了一種核心向外分支的設計。

各個病房的採光，主要是借助立面的設計。建築師利用建築角度的原理，把陽光從鋪砌在室內的白色瓷磚上，散射到建築物的各部份，醫院的正面亦設有簡潔的遮陽裝置。

醫院的中央部份為建築物的主幹，採用玻璃磚及帽狀屋頂潤飾其頂部。為了降低對比，四座側翼的末端會向內收窄，並在頂部設置一個帽狀屋頂，及以半圓形的窗口設計作點綴。

建築物外，一條顏色濃淡相宜的透明有蓋行人道，穿過綠化園景，到達醫院大樓入口的庭院。入口庭院更設有一個格框上蓋，與四周景色互相呼應。

2

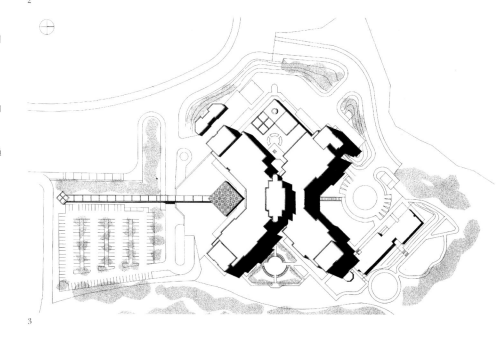

3

4

5

6

7

8

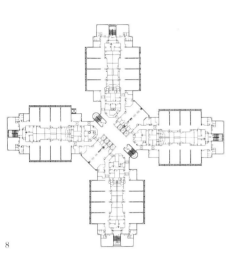

9

10

North District Hospital

Design/Completion 1994/1997
Fanling, New Territories, Hong Kong
Hospital Authority
63,000 square metres
Reinforced concrete post and beam
Ceramic mosaic tiles, aluminium curtain wall

北區醫院

設計年份/完成年份：1994年/1997年
香港新界粉嶺
醫院管理局
建築面積：63,000平方米
建築結構：鋼筋混凝土柱樑結構
建築材料：瓷磚牆身、鋁質幕牆

1

This seven-storey district hospital is the first design and build healthcare facility commissioned by the client. An acute hospital, it comprises 618 beds with standard support departments and staff accommodation. Ambulatory care facilities are also provided by the specialist out-patient clinic, day procedure centre, psychiatric and geriatric day hospitals.

Apart from enhancing and developing the elevational treatment, the design team has deviated little from the original concept produced by the Hospital Authority. The plan establishes a hospital street with ward-housing departments branching off from the central spine. This arrangement results in an irregular overall massing.

The elevation is interpreted as horizontal layers, with the first layer centred on columns which open up the ground floor area to the external landscaping. This movement continues up the facade, with the top layer recessed and capped to break down the scale.

All of the circulation cores, which are positioned on the sides of the attached blocks, are similarly accented with glass and coloured walls in a formal reworking of the classical pillar concept.

The front entrance is expressed through two adjacent elements which form a vast, curvilinear canopy. The whole is clad in aluminium.

北區醫院這所七層高的分區醫院是第一所由醫院管理局委託承建商以「設計及建築」的合約形式興建的醫療設施。醫院內設有618張病床，並且備有急症服務、高水準支援部門及醫護人員宿舍。除住院服務外，該醫院亦透過各專科診部、日間醫療中心、精神科日間醫院以及老人日間醫院，提供非住院服務。

在體現及設計醫院大樓之過程中，建築師盡量保持醫管局原有之運作概念。在平面佈置上，大樓主體以由東至西之中央通道形成一條「醫院街」，而各醫療部門便從「醫院街」分支出來成為附樓，產生一種總體集合而不規則的效果。

建築師亦仔細處理醫院大樓立體效果及美感。大樓的底層以柱體為主，令柱樑結構更能顯現，亦使外圍景觀與室內互相呼應。這種設計形式將繼續向上發展，但到了頂層便會向內收窄及加設飛簷和帽狀屋頂，使龐大的立面看起來像縮細了一樣。

所有建築物的樓梯，均設於各座附樓的側面，設計師並以玻璃及色彩多變的牆壁加強其形態，承接古典的柱體概念。而醫院正面入口則由兩個彎曲的巨型頂篷連接組成，並以鋁鍍面。

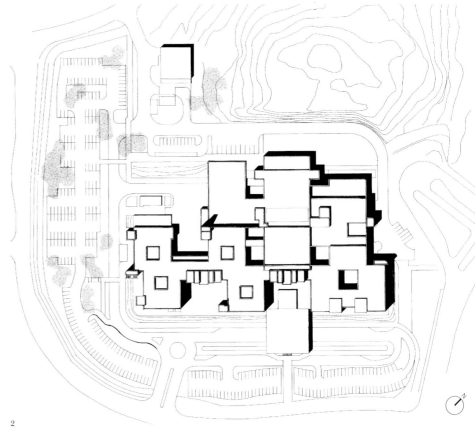

2

3

4

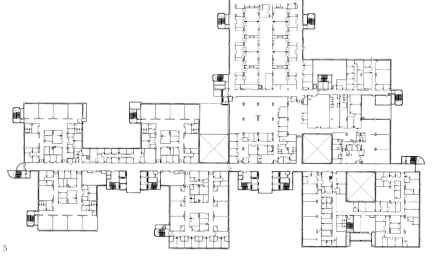

5

8

6

9

7

10

Haven of Hope Hospital Redevelopment

Design/Completion 1992/1997
Tseung Kwan O, New Territories, Hong Kong
Haven of Hope Christian Service
26,000 square metres
Reinforced concrete column and beam
Ceramic mosaic tiles

靈實醫院重建計劃

設計年份 / 完成年份：1992 年 /1997 年
香港新界將軍澳
基督教靈實協會
建築面積：26,000 平方米
建築結構：鋼筋混凝土柱樑結構
建築材料：彩色瓷磚

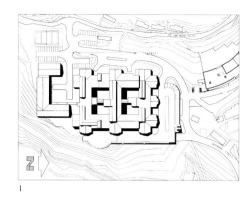

1

The redevelopment works included the demolition of the existing family quarters and administration buildings and the construction of a low-rise, non-acute hospital with 316 beds. In-house support services include occupational therapy, physiotherapy, clinical pathology and linguistic therapy. There is also a low-rise annex building housing a nursing school, pupil nursing, various staff accommodation and a staff kitchen/canteen.

A major influence on the design was the need for the hospital to conform to the profile of the naturally landscaped 70,000-square-metre site. The hospital itself is subject to horizontal planning based on a "hospital street" concept with "plug-in" departments organised in a cruciform for maximum flexibility.

Four green-roofed, landscaped courtyards form the basis of the plan, recalling a traditional Chinese village. These courtyards introduce natural light and fresh air to the complex. Vertical and horizontal elements on the elevation break down the building's scale and shade the rooms within. The hospital rises in steps from three to six storeys, its terraced form relating to the natural contours of the site. Verdant roof gardens complement the village aesthetic.

The hospital buildings stand on a two-storey podium which is manifestly different in character, suggesting a medieval castle and moat. The podium houses workshops, storage facilities and a car park.

該項重建工程包括拆除舊有家庭宿舍及行政樓，興建一座設有316個床位的低層治療慢性病的醫院。醫院內設立的支援服務包括：職業治療部、物理治療部、臨床病理學部，以及語言治療部。另外，還有一座低層附樓，內設一所護理學校、學護及各職系職員之宿舍、職員廚房及餐廳。

影響工程設計的重大因素是該醫院的外觀。建築師需要與面積為70,000平方米的自然景觀區與醫院互相呼應。醫院本身以醫療街的平面概念為基礎，加上以十字形佈局規劃各個部門，以取得最大的靈活性。

翠綠的屋頂與景觀化的庭院，構成該項重建工程的基調，使人聯想起傳統的中國村落。庭院把自然光及新鮮空氣引進醫院大樓。大樓立面上的垂直及水平構件，使大樓的比例降低，並使陽光不會直射樓內的房間。醫院以台級式分佈，由三層遞增至六層，與座落地點周圍的自然輪廓融洽相襯。翠綠的屋頂配合庭院花園，使醫院洋溢著鄉 村美麗的景色。

醫院大樓建立在一座兩層高的平台底座上，使建築物尤如置身於翠綠山巒中的城堡。平台底座內設有各類工場、貯物室和停車場。

2

3

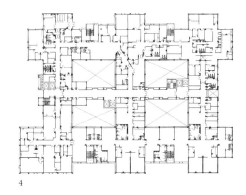

4

5

6

7

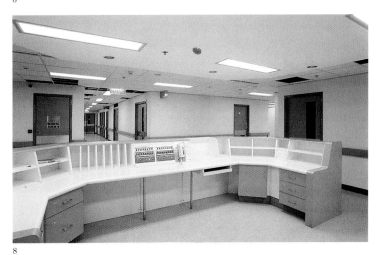

8

9

Tseung Kwan O Hospital

Design/Completion 1995/1999
Tseung Kwan O, New Territories, Hong Kong
Hospital Authority
Reinforced concrete post and beam
Ceramic mosaic tiles, aluminium curtain wall

將軍澳醫院

設計年份 / 完成年份：1995 年 /1999 年
香港新界將軍澳
醫院管理局
建築結構：鋼筋混凝土柱樑結構
建築材料：彩色瓷磚、鋁質幕牆

1

This acute general hospital with 458 beds and advanced day treatment facilities is the result of an enhanced design and build contract. Ambulatory care services represent a sizeable component of the facility, providing day surgery, day care, out-patient and community services. The hospital also delivers 24-hour accident and emergency services, with a further 14 beds. In addition, all major specialities will be available.

The approach to the hospital is bifurcated; entry can be made on either of two levels which converge at the central core. A sweeping driveway passes through palm-treed gardens to an impressive curved entrance with columns. A bus terminal is located on the lower level, giving access to a five-storey skylit atrium.

The hospital's unusual blueprint is the product of deft juxtapositions of geometric forms. A standard, rectangular block stands at the head of a central core from which extend three narrow arms; one side of each arm is dramatically skewed.

Great expanses of glass and curtain wall features punctuate the stark white skin of the exterior. Verdant terraces and green-tiled roofs add further ornament.

將軍澳醫院是一所設有急症室服務的全科醫院，擁有 458個病床及先進的日間診治設施，並採用設計及建築合約形式興建。該醫院擁有寬敞位置提供各項醫療護理服務、日間手術、日間護理、門診及社區服務。醫院亦為市民提供24小時急症服務，另外亦設有14個急症病床及提供各種主要專科醫療服務。

醫院設有兩個位於不同層數入口，通往醫院中央位置。一條彎彎的車道貫穿種滿棕櫚樹的花園，加上入口壯觀的柱作配襯，令人留下難忘的印象。巴士總站設於醫院低層，可由此進入一個五層高的天窗前庭。

該院的設計特色，在於建築物幾何形狀的巧妙佈置，中心外型方正的大樓向外伸展出三個側翼，做成三個斜面。

建築師更採用了大面積的方形玻璃和幕牆，點綴大樓樸素的白色外牆。多個青翠的平台和斜面屋頂設計，亦為醫院外觀增添幾分動人色彩。

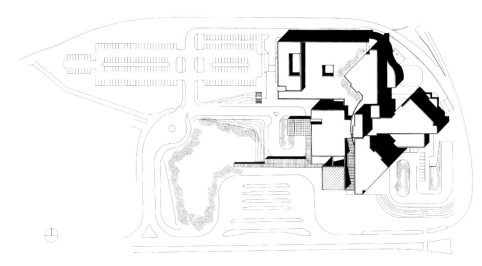

2

3

1　Interior perspective
2　Site plan
3　Model view
4　Typical ward
5　Section
6　Central nursing stations facilitate ease of supervision
7　Typical floor plan
8　View of interior terracing
9　Atrium view showing stepped floors

1　室內透視圖
2　位置圖
3　模型
4　標準病房
5　剖面圖
6　護士當值處設於中央位置，方便察看各病房情況
7　標準平面圖
8　室內呈階梯狀的設計
9　天井映照下的階梯狀地台

4

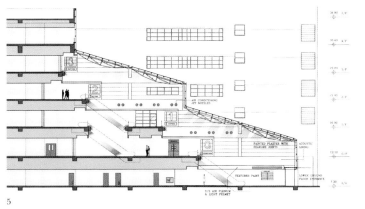

5

8

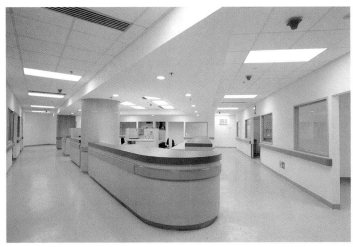

6

7

9

Cheng Yan Ying, Grace 鄭恩鎣; Kwan Wing Hong, Dominic 關永康; Ng Wing Shun, Anthony Vincent 吳永順

Kwan Wing Hong, Dominic
BArch (HK), HKIA, RIBA, RAIA Registered Architect,
Authorised Person (Architect)

Dominic Kwan is the founder of a thriving local architectural practice which has made significant contributions to Hong Kong's built environment.

After graduating from the University of Hong Kong in 1972, Dominic went on to work for several architectural firms and the Hong Kong Public Works Department.

From 1976 to 1978, he had the unique opportunity to lead Sun Hung Kai's architectural design team and contribute to the formulation of the development strategy. T.S. Kwok, accompanied by Dominic, toured potential development sites in Hong Kong. Such excursions were the prelude to intensive brainstorming sessions during which strategic options were examined and potential schemes formulated. This insight into how the "client" operates has proven invaluable to his subsequent career.

In 1979, Dominic became one of the founding directors of KNW Architects & Engineers Limited. Thanks to accomplished direction, the firm received HKIA recognition: the Silver Medal for Excellence in 1983, 1984 and 1989; and the Diploma of Merit in 1987. After the restructuring of KNW in 1991, Dominic established Kwan & Associates Architects Ltd. There was little need for reorganisation, as most of the staff stayed to complete ongoing assignments.

The firm's reputation for skilled design and efficient project management has produced an impressive portfolio which includes the design of Island Place, Salisbury Garden Shopping Complex, Ko Shan Theatre improvements, and the University of Hong Kong Phase 5.

A joint venture with Percy Thomas Partnership (Hong Kong) Ltd in 1987 produced an offshoot firm, Kwan-PTP, which provides comprehensive healthcare design services to both public and private sector clients. Naturally, Dominic is a director of Kwan-PTP. Principal projects undertaken by Kwan-PTP include North District, Tai Po, Haven of Hope, and Tseung Kwan O hospitals and the Hong Kong University New Medical Faculty Complex.

In 1995, Dominic was made chief executive of PTP and this appointment has strengthened the relationship between the companies.

關永康

香港大學建築學士，香港建築師學會會員，英國皇家建築師學會會員，
澳洲皇家建築師學會會員，香港註冊建築師，認可人士（建築師）

關永康先生是關永康建築師有限公司的創辦人，對香港建築設計業貢獻良多。

關先生在一九七二年畢業於香港大學，繼而在多間建築師樓及香港政府工務局工作。

一九七六年至一九七八年間，關永康先生曾在新鴻基地產有限公司郭得勝先生下服務，從而洞悉發展商客戶的獨特見解，對開發日後的發展有重大影響。

一九七九年，關永康先生與他人創辦了「關吳黃建築師 • 工程師有限公司」，在他們的傑出領導下，公司分別獲得香港建築師學會所頒發的一九八三年、一九八四年和一九八九年的優秀建築設計銀獎，以及一九八七年的建築設計優異獎。關吳黃於一九九一年重組，關永康先生在此時創立了關永康建築師有限公司，而公司內部並沒有太大變動，因為大部份員工均願意留下，繼續合作完成各項工程。

關永康建築師有限公司專業化的建築設計，以及高效率的工程管理質素為該公司建立良好的聲譽。其出色的建築設計作品包括港運城、尖沙咀名店城及梳士巴利公園、高山劇場擴建工程以及香港大學第五期工程等。

一九八七年，關永康建築師有限公司與唐謀士建築設計事務所合作成立了關永康 - 唐謀士建築師 • 醫院設計師有限公司，關永康先生並擔任董事一職。該公司專門為公營及私人機構提供全面的醫療設施設計服務，包括北區醫院、大埔醫院、靈實醫院、將軍澳醫院及香港大學新醫學院綜合大樓。

一九九五年，關永康先生獲委任為唐謀士建築師 • 醫院設計師有限公司的執行總監。進一步加強了關永康建築師有限公司與唐謀士建築師 • 醫院設計師有限公司之間的合作關係。

Vincent Ng

Ng Wing Shun, Anthony Vincent
BA(AS)(Hons), BArch(Dist), M.Urban Design(HK), HKIA, RIBA, RAIA
Registered Architect, Authorised Person (Architect)

After graduating from the University of Hong Kong, Vincent Ng joined KNW Architects & Engineers Limited in 1985. He has subsequently worked his way up to become director-in-charge of three architectural teams at Kwan & Associates Architects Ltd, with major architectural and urban design projects including the Island Place Commercial and Residential Development, the KCRC West Rail Project TS-100, the planning study for NW Lantau, the University of Hong Kong Phase 5 Redevelopment, the New World Hotel renovation, St Francis Church, Ma On Shan, improvements to Ko Shan Theatre, the Nursing Home Development at Haven of Hope Hospital, and Chek Lap Kok Telephone Exchange.

Vincent was made an associate in 1989, a senior associate (Kwan & Associates) in 1991, a deputy director in 1993, and a director in 1994. This was also the year in which he was presented with the prestigious Young Architect (Hong Kong) Award.

In 1995, Vincent became a director of Percy Thomas Partnership (Hong Kong) with responsibility for developing the company's public works commissions. Vincent is also a director of Kwan-PTP.

Vincent has been a guest critic in the architectural design studios at both the University of Hong Kong and the Chinese University of Hong Kong.

吳永順
香港大學建築學文學士，香港大學建築學士，香港大學城市設計碩士，
香港建築師學會會員，英國皇家建築師學會會員，澳洲皇家建築師學會會員，
香港註冊建築師，認可人士(建築師)

吳永順先生畢業於香港大學，於一九八五年加入關吳黃建築師●工程師
有限公司，並分別於一九八九年及一九九一年成為合伙人及高級合伙人。
其後關吳黃改組成為關永康建築師有限公司，吳永順出任該公司的副董事，
於一九九四年獲擢升為執行董事，並於同年獲頒發香港傑出青年建築師獎
的殊榮。

他領導三個建築設計組的工作，所負責的主要建築及城市設計工程項目
包括：馬來西亞銀行新加坡總部大廈、港運城商業及住宅樓宇發展計劃、
九廣鐵路西鐵工程TS-100、大嶼山西北部規劃研究、香港大學第五期
重建工程、新世界酒店改建工程、馬鞍山聖芳濟教堂、高山劇場擴建工程、
靈實醫院護理安老院發展計劃以及赤鱲角電話機樓等。

在建築教育方面，吳永順亦以客座評論家的身份，參與香港大學及香港
中文大學建築設計工作室的教學工作。

一九九五年，吳永順獲委任為唐謀士建築設計事務所的董事，負責發展
公司的公共建築工程。另外，他亦是關永康-唐謀士建築師●醫院設計師有
限公司的董事。

Grace Cheng

Cheng Yan Ying, Grace
AADipl, HKIA, RIBA,
Registered Architect, Authorised Person (Architect)

Grace Cheng has played a principal part in the design of a number of key buildings for Kwan & Associates Ltd. Grace joined the then KNW Architects & Engineers Limited as an associate in 1985, and was responsible for detailed design work and administration for various residential and commercial projects.

In 1991, Grace was appointed senior associate of the newly formed Kwan & Associates Architects Ltd and was made a director in 1993. She is now director-in-charge of three architectural teams and her current major projects include: the MTRC Kowloon Station Development; the Discovery Bay North Development; Palace Mall underground shopping centre at Salisbury Garden; the Chung On Terrace residential development; the Housing Society Sandwich Class development; the New World Centre Hotel extension, and the Hing Wai Building.

In 1995, Grace was appointed a director of Percy Thomas Partnership (Hong Kong) with a mandate to develop the company's commercial sector work. Grace is also a director of Kwan-PTP.

鄭恩瑩
英國倫敦建築學院文憑，香港建築師學會會員，英國皇家建築師學會會員，
香港註冊建築師，認可人士(建築師)

鄭恩瑩於一九八五年成為關吳黃建築師•工程師有限公司的合伙人，負責各項住宅及商業建築項目的設計及行政工作，於一九九一年獲新成立的關永康建築師有限公司委任為高級合伙人，並於一九九三年正式成為該公司的董事。

現時，她領導三個建築設計組的工作，處理多項重要的建築設計工程，其中包括：機鐵九龍車站發展計劃第一期、愉景灣北部擴建計劃、尖沙咀名店城及梳士巴利園、中安台住宅發展計劃、房屋協會夾心階層住屋計劃、新世界中心酒店擴建計劃及中環興瑋大廈重建等。

一九九五年，鄭恩瑩獲委任為唐謀士建築設計事務所的董事，負責發展該公司的商業部份工作。另外，她亦是關永康-唐謀士建築師•醫院設計師有限公司的董事。

Staff List

公司組織

Directors

Kwan Wing Hong, Dominic; Ng Wing Shun, Anthony Vincent; Cheng Yan Ying, Grace

Deputy Directors

Lam Chung Wai, Tony; Tsang Wai Yin, Michael

Senior Associates & Associates

Law Chi Yung, Andrew; Lui Ann; Lee Siu Cheung, Marco; Wong Man Sang, Vincent; Wong Ming Tei, Edward; Au Long Hin, Aubrey; Wong Chi Kin, Kenneth; Wong Hon Keung, Max; Lui Cheuk Ho, Ronson; Wong Kwok Hing, Dominic; Kwok Yat Lung, Joseph; Chow Wing Keung, Lambert; Chiang Wai Leung, Bobby; Ng Ching Hong, Arthur

Architects

Chan Yuen On, Patrick; Law Fat Lai, James; Leung Sai Ho, Edward; Ng Hin, Felix; Kwok Ka Chun, Peter; Lee Tsup Chung, Anthony; Lam Hei, Lawrance; Leung Franklin Eli; Ho Man Chuen, Anthony

Supporting Staff

Kwok Yui Chung, Danny; Hung Hing Yuen, Henry; Mak Chung Kit, Lawrence; Lee Chun Kau, Paul; Cheung Chi Wai, Andy; Man Kam Hung, Ricky; Kwong Kwok Tung, Vincent; Fung Man Kit; Chung Man Shun, Matthew; Yeung Chi Hung, Wallace; Tse Kam Wing; Kwok Tung Wai, Richard; Leung King Tong, Tommy; Tam Chiu Kit, Danny; Li Yat Ming; Yeung Wing Tong; Cheuk Yat Man, Simon; Wu Kui Wah, Sammy; Kwok Yung Yeuk, Jeff; Kwok Hon Po, Anthony; Leung Kwok Yiu, Stephen; Mak Kwok Ping, Tony; Ma Leung Kee, Danny; Yu Keng Po; Yiu Leung Ping, Wallace; Tsui Chi Keung, Joseph; Lai Kwong Wing; Lau Ka Hung, Remos; Chui Chi Ming, Marco; Wan Lap Pui, Julian; Chan Po Ming, Tonnis; Yuen Chi Keung, Elson; Tam Ping Ngok, Stephen; Lam Siu Chuen; Tam Wing Kin, Jacky; Tam Tin Long, Leo; Lai Cheong Sing; Chan Kwok Hung, Wilson; Kwong Chi Shing; Tse Lung Fai, Dee; Tao Kwai Cheung, Den; Muk Man Lok, Ken; Chan King Tak, Dick; Yeung Man Tak, Leo; Leung Chi Hung, Calvin; Wong Ho Yin, Stephen; Tam Lok Tim; Fung Wing Kai, Guy; Kwok Chun Wing, Alan; Leung Wai Kay; Woo Kwok Fat, Jeff; Tsui Chi Ming, Vincent; Chung Wai Kwong, Ellis; Wong Ka Ning, Alan; Leung Mo Kit, Fifi; Chau Yuen Tak, Carrie; Tang Ka Fai; Lau Tat Chi, Ricky; Li Loi Hing; Lau Kai Cheong; Chan Pui Lun; Kwok Sui Kee; Kei Sai Kwong; Wong Tak Fai; Chung Ping Fai, Dickson; Ip Siu Kay, Tony; Yip Chun Hung; Tse Jick Ting; Ma Yiu Chuen, Andrew; Yau Pui Ching; Wong Chi Wing, Albert; Cheung Sze Wai, Celia; Ho Po Lin, Fiona; Leong Choi Mui, May; Cheung Wai Cheong, Jones; Fung Sau Wah, Winnie; Luk Mi Kuen, Eva; Chan Shuk Fan, Sonia; Wong Suk Chun, Betty; Cheung Sau King, Carol; Cheung, Jovy; Tsang Shui Ping, Apple; Cheung Kit Ming; Luk Ka Man, Carmen; Lee Oi Yee, Kennex; Chan Siu Fung, Fanny; Tsang Hung Mui, Aries; Wong So Ngor, Anna; Leung Yin Lee, Moon; Yau Wan Ying, Mabel; Pou Mei Ling, Miranda; Ma Man Kuen, Shirley; Lee Pik Yiu, Patty; Mok Yee Wa, Joy; Lee Mee Ling, Kitty; Yueng Wai Ling, Jenny; Chan Kwai Ling, Ken; Pun Noi Fun, Marina; Chim Kwai Yung; Cheung Kung Wai; Ngo Tai Leung, Jim; Fu Siu Hung, April; Lam Siu Po; Chui Wing Lok; Chiu Yuk Lin, May; Chan Wai Man, Raymond; Li Kin Pan, Stanley; Chan Chun Sun, Sunny; Pang Ching Man, Daniel; Chan Kim Wah; Lau Wai Shun, Peter; Lee Hing Lung, Joshua; Wong Chi Chung, Ivan

董事

關永康, 吳永順, 鄭恩瑩

副董事

林中偉, 曾偉賢

高級主任建築師及主任建築師

羅致勇, 呂藹, 李兆祥, 黃文生, 黃明悌, 區朗軒, 黃智健, 黃漢強, 雷卓浩, 王國興, 郭一龍, 周永強, 蔣偉亮, 吳靖康

建築師

陳源安, 羅發禮, 梁世豪, 吳衍, 郭家俊, 李執中, 林晞, 梁以立, 何敏泉

工作人員

郭銳忠, 孔慶元, 麥中傑, 李震球, 張志偉, 文錦洪, 酈國棟, 馮文傑, 鍾萬信, 楊志鴻, 謝錦榮, 郭棟威, 梁景堂, 譚超傑, 李一明, 楊永棠, 卓一民, 胡鉅華, 郭榕躍, 郭漢波, 梁國堯, 麥國平, 馬亮奇, 余鏡波, 姚良平, 徐志強, 黎廣華, 劉家鴻, 徐志明, 溫立培, 陳寶明, 袁智強, 譚秉鍔, 林兆全, 譚永健, 譚天明, 黎昌盛, 陳國雄, 酈志成, 謝龍輝, 杜桂祥, 穆民樂, 陳景德, 楊萬德, 梁志鴻, 王浩然, 譚樂添, 馮穎佳, 郭俊榮, 梁偉基, 吳國發, 徐志明, 鍾偉光, 黃家寧, 梁慕潔, 周婉德, 鄧家輝, 劉達志, 李來興, 劉啟昌, 陳沛倫, 郭瑞基, 紀世光, 黃德輝, 鍾炳輝, 葉肇祺, 葉振洪, 謝植庭, 馬耀泉, 遊珮貞, 黃熾榮, 張思慧, 何寶蓮, 梁翠梅, 張偉昌, 馮秀華, 陸美娟, 陳淑芬, 黃淑珍, 張秀瓊, 張雅芬, 曾瑞萍, 張潔明, 陸嘉雯, 李靄儀, 陳少鳳, 曾紅梅, 黃素娥, 梁燕莉, 邱蘊瑩, 鮑美玲, 馬文娟, 李璧瑤, 莫綺華, 李美玲, 楊惠玲, 陳桂寧, 潘耐寬, 詹桂容, 張公慰, 敖大諒, 傅小紅, 林小波, 徐永樂, 趙玉蓮, 陳偉民, 李健彬, 陳俊榮, 彭程萬, 陳劍華, 劉維信, 李慶隆, 黃志忠

Selected works by Category 項目分類

Commercial 商業項目

Airport Railway Kowloon Station Development - Master Planning & Design, Kowloon
九龍站地鐵上蓋發展計劃 — 總規劃設計

Great Western Plaza, Kennedy Town, Hong Kong
香港堅尼地城Great Western Plaza

New World Hotel Renovation, Tsimshatsui, Kowloon
九龍尖沙咀新世界酒店裝修工程

Commercial Development at Corner of Tin Hau Temple Road / Tung Lo Wan Road, Hong Kong
香港銅鑼灣百樂戲院重建計劃

Hing Wai Building, Central, Hong Kong
香港中環興瑋大廈

P.J. Plaza, Causeway Bay, Hong Kong
香港銅鑼灣翡翠明珠廣場

Development of Mass Transit Railway Island Line - Causeway Bay East Concourse, Hong Kong*
香港地下鐵路發展計劃 — 港島線銅鑼灣東部聯線發展

Island Centre, Causeway Bay, Hong Kong*
香港銅鑼灣金堡中心

Proposed Development of Maybank Chambers, Singapore
新加坡馬來亞銀行總部大廈發展計劃

Development of Mass Transit Railway Tsuen Wan Depot (Nan Fung Centre), New Territories*
新界地下鐵路荃灣總站 (南豐中心)

Island Place, North Point, Hong Kong
香港北角港運城

Proposed Hotel Development at IL.2609, Causeway Bay, Hong Kong
香港銅鑼灣2609地段酒店發展計劃

East Point Centre, Causeway Bay, Hong Kong*
香港銅鑼灣東角中心

Kennedy Town Centre, Kennedy Town, Hong Kong
香港堅尼地城堅城中心

Proposed Hotel Development at Tai Shue Wan Site, Aberdeen, Hong Kong
香港香港仔大樹灣酒店發展計劃

EDSA Commercial Complex, Philippines*
菲律賓馬尼拉EDSA商業中心

New World Extension, Central, Hong Kong
香港中環新世界大廈擴建工程

Proposed LDC Scheme at Waterloo Road / Yunnan Lane, Kowloon
九龍窩打老道/雲南里LDC發展計劃

Extension to New World Centre, Tsimshatsui, Kowloon
九龍尖沙咀新世界中心擴建工程

New World Hotel, Metro Manila, Philippines*
菲律賓馬尼拉新世界酒店

Redevelopment of Methodist Church, Wanchai, Hong Kong
香港灣仔循道衛理聯合教會香港堂重建計劃

Commercial 商業項目

Renovation of Bond Theatre, Kwun Tong, Kowloon
九龍觀塘寶聲戲院改建工程

St. John's Building and Lower Peak Tram Terminal, Central, Hong Kong*
香港中環聖約翰大廈及花園道纜車站

Yam Tze Commercial Building, Wanchai, Hong Kong
香港灣仔壬子商業大廈

Salisbury Garden / Palace Mall, Tsimshatsui, Kowloon
九龍梳士巴利花園/名店城

The Goldmark, Causeway Bay, Hong Kong*
香港銅鑼灣黃金廣場

Yan's Tower, Aberdeen, Hong Kong
香港香港仔甄占記大廈

Residential 住宅項目

8A Stanley Beach Road, Stanley, Hong Kong*
香港赤柱灘道8A

Belleview Drive, Repulse Bay, Hong Kong*
香港淺水灣麗景道

Discovery Bay North Development - Phase 10, Lantau Island, New Territories
新界愉景灣北 — 第十期

Airport Railway Kowloon Station Development - First Development Package, Kowloon
九龍站地鐵上蓋發展計劃 — First Development Package

Broadview Garden, Tsing Yi, New Territories
新界青衣島偉景花園

Discovery Bay North Development - N1a, Lantau Island, New Territories
新界愉景灣北 — N1a

Airport Railway Kowloon Station Development - Master Planning & Design, Kowloon
九龍站地鐵上蓋發展計劃 — 總規劃設計

Chevalier Garden, Shatin, New Territories*
新界沙田富安花園

Discovery Bay - N1b, Lantau Island, New Territories
新界愉景灣北 — N1b

Banyan Villa, Stanley, Hong Kong*
香港赤柱榕蔭園

Discovery Bay North Development - Master Layout Plan 6.0, Lantau Island, New Territories
新界愉景灣北 — 總規劃

Greenpark Villa, Fanling, New Territories
新界粉嶺蔚翠花園

Residential 住宅項目

Galesend, 6 Bluff Path,
The Peak, Hong Kong*
香港山頂百祿徑6號

Residential Development at
Chung On Terrace,
North Point, Hong Kong
香港北角中安台住宅
重建計劃

Sandwich Class Housing
Project at Perowne Barracks,
Tuen Mun, New Territories
新界屯門夾心階層住屋計劃

Hill Top Gardens,
Hammer Hill, Kowloon*
九龍海港花園

Residential Development at
Hung Shui Kiu,
New Territories
新界洪水橋住宅發展計劃

Stanley Court, Stanley,
Hong Kong*
香港赤柱海灣園

Island Place, North Point,
Hong Kong
香港北角港運城

Residential Development at
Mining Lot 20 and NKIL 5910
Cha Kwo Ling, New Territories
九龍茶果嶺住宅發展計劃

Staff Quarters at
Shaw Brothers Studio,
Clear Water Bay, Kowloon
九龍清水灣邵氏兄弟
有限公司職員宿舍

Mt. Parker Lodge, Quarry Bay,
Hong Kong*
香港鰂魚涌康景花園

Residential Development at
Ngai Chi Wan, Kowloon
九龍牛池灣住宅發展計劃

TS100 Kam Tin Station
Property Development,
New Territories
新界錦田站地鐵TS100上蓋
發展計劃

Pristine Villa, Shatin,
New Territories
新界沙田曉翠山莊

Residential Development at
Tai Po Town Lot 139, Tai Po,
New Territories
新界大埔139地段商住
綜合大廈

Tsui Chuk Garden,
Wong Tai Sin, Kowloon
九龍黃大仙翠竹花園

Proposed Redevelopment of
KMB Depot, Lai Chi Kok,
Kowloon
九龍荔枝角九龍巴士廠
發展計劃

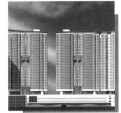
Residential Development at
Yuen Long CDA,
New Territories
新界元朗綜合發展區住宅
發展計劃

Tsui Lai Garden, Sheung
Shui, New Territories*
新界上水翠麗花園

Repulse Bay Hotel
Redevelopment, Repulse Bay,
Hong Kong*
香港淺水灣酒店重建計劃

Sandwich Class Housing at
29 Ka Wai Man Road,
Kennedy Town, Hong Kong
香港堅尼地城加惠民道29號
夾心階層住屋計劃

Yuk Ming Court, Sheung Wan,
Hong Kong
香港上環毓明閣

Industrial 工貿項目

Agincourt Industrial Building, Yau Tong, Kowloon*
九龍油塘白宜工業大廈

Godown Development at Tuen Mun 379 , New Territories
新界屯門379貨倉發展計劃

Redevelopment of 11-17 Kok Cheung Street, Tai Kok Tsui, Kowloon
九龍大角咀角祥街11-17號重建計劃

Chek Lap Kok Telephone Exchange, New Territories
新界赤鱲角電話機樓

New Headquarters Building for Dragonair and CNAC at Chek Lap Kok Design Competition, New Territories
新界赤鱲角港龍航空及中國民航總部大樓之設計競賽

Yee Kuk Industrial Centre, Cheung Sha Wan, Kowloon
九龍長沙灣怡高工業中心

Factory/ Office Building at Tung Chau Street, Cheung Sha Wan, Kowloon
九龍長沙灣通州街工貿中心

On Lok Exchange, Hong Kong Telephone Company, Fanling, New Territories*
新界粉嶺安樂村電話機樓

Yuen Fat Wharf & Godown, Cheung Sha Wan, Kowloon
九龍長沙灣新潤發倉庫碼頭

Hospital 醫院項目

Adventist Hospital, Central, Hong Kong
香港中環港安醫院

Haven of Hope Hospital , Tseung Kwan O, New Territories
九龍將軍澳靈實醫院

Nursing Home Development, Haven of Hope Hospital, Tseung Kwan O, New Territories
九龍將軍澳靈實護理安老院

Canadian International Hospital and Technology Exchange Centre, Aberdeen, Hong Kong
香港香港仔加拿大國際醫院暨技術交流中心

New Medical Complex, The University of Hong Kong, Pokfulam, Hong Kong
香港薄扶林香港大學新醫學院綜合大樓

Tai Po Hospital, New Territories
新界大埔醫院

Geriatric Day Hospital at Wong Tai Sin Hospital, Kowloon
九龍黃大仙醫院何淑媛紀念老人日間醫院

North District Hospital, Sheung Shui, New Territories
新界粉嶺北區醫院

Tseung Kwan O Hospital, New Territories
九龍將軍澳醫院

Institutional 公共機構項目

Additional Indoor Games Hall at Boundary Street, Mongkok, Kowloon*
九龍旺角界限街第二號室內運動場

Improvement Works to Ko Shan Theatre, Hung Hom, Kowloon
九龍紅磡高山劇場擴建工程

St. Francis Church at Ma On Shan, New Territories
新界沙田天主教馬鞍山聖方濟堂

Canossian Convent Primary and Secondary School, Quarry Bay, Hong Kong*
香港鰂魚涌嘉諾撒小學及中學

Interior Fitting Out Works for Star of the Sea Church, Wanchai, Hong Kong
香港柴灣海星堂室內設計

St. Joan of Arc Secondary School, North Point, Hong Kong*
香港北角聖貞德學校中學部

Extension to Student Hostel 2, The Chinese Univesity of Hong Kong, Shatin, New Territories
新界沙田香港中文大學學生宿舍擴建工程

Kowloon Bay Sports Ground, Kowloon*
九龍九龍灣運動場

To Kwa Wan Indoor Games Hall, Kowloon*
九龍土瓜灣遊樂場

Fat Hing Street, Playground, Sheung Wan, Hong Kong*
香港上環發興街遊樂場

New Administration Headquarters for Tung Wah Group of Hospitals, Sheung Wan, Hong Kong*
香港上環東華三院行政大樓

Tung Wah Group of Hospitals Jockey Club Care & Attention Home for the Elderly, Sandy Bay, Hong Kong
香港大口環東華三院馬會護理安老院

Honeyville Canossian Retreat House, Mount Davis, Hong Kong*
香港摩星嶺嘉諾撒靜修院

Sai Yee Street Garden & Public Toilet, Mongkok, Kowloon*
九龍旺角洗衣街公園

University of Hong Kong Phase V Redevelopment, Pokfulam, Hong Kong
香港薄扶林香港大學第五期教學大廈

Hong Kong Institute of Biotechnology, Shatin, New Territories
新界沙田香港生物科技研究院

Post-Graduate Hostel, Chinese University of Hong Kong, Shatin, New Territories
新界沙田香港中文大學研究生宿舍

Villa Maddalena, Macau*
澳門瑪大肋納安老院

China 國內項目

Agile Hotel, Zhongshan
中山雅居樂酒店

Beijing Kuan Lun Hotel, Beijing*
北京崑崙飯店

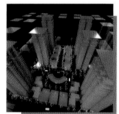

Block 116 of Taipingqao Development, Luwan District, Shanghai
上海市盧灣區太平橋116地區 住宅發展計劃

Guilin Athletic Hotel, Guilin*
桂林體育賓館

Hong Jiang Plaza at Jiangmen
江門市鴻江廣場

Kunming Changchun Lu Commercial Development, Kunming
昆明市長春路商業發展計劃

Mao Er Dao Holiday Resort, Chengdu
四川貓兒島渡假村

Nanjing Tong Lu Commercial Development, Shanghai
上海市南京東路商業 發展計劃

Nation Wealth Plaza, Beijing
北京台友廣場

Proposed Commercial Development at Hoi Nam Province
海南島台育中心商業 發展計劃

Proposed Comprehensive Development at Huizhou
惠州綜合發展計劃

Proposed Commercial Development at Jiading, Shanghai
上海市嘉定頂峰廣場 發展計劃

Proposed Comprehensive Development at Ren Min Nan Lu on Lot No. 87, Wu Hou Qu, Chengdu
成都台育花園綜合發展計劃

Proposed Hotel Development at Lucky Target Square, Shanghai
上海市峻岭廣場酒店綜合 發展計劃

Proposed Office and Apartment at Chang Jiang Road, Dalian
大連長江路商住綜合 發展計劃

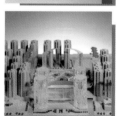

Shantou World Trade Centre, Hantou
汕頭市汕頭世界貿易中心

Shenyang Plaza, Shenyang
瀋陽市瀋陽廣場

Tai Yu Square, Beijing
北京台友廣場

* Projects before 1991 and practising as KNW Architects & Engineers Ltd.
由關吳黃建築師・工程師有限公司自一九九一年以前負責之項目

Index

索引

KWAN
ARCHITECTS

KWAN & ASSOCIATES ARCHITECTS LTD 關永康建築師有限公司

10/F, Island Place Tower, 510 King's Road, North Point, Hong Kong.   Tel : 2880 1128   Fax : 2811 0780   Email : kwanarch@kwanarch.com

香港北角英皇道510號港運大廈十樓   電話 : 2880 1128   圖文傳真 : 2811 0780   電子郵件 : kwanarch@kwanarch.com